Granda

Contains strong la
and scene

Peter Flint

The story, characters, organisations, and situations herein contained are entirely fictitious. Any similarities to any person(s) (living, dead...*or otherwise*) or organisations, is completely coincidental and entirely unintentional. The views and opinions expressed by the characters are not representative of the author(s) or Nemesis Publishing.

All categories are assigned subject to Nemesis Publishing policy and are provided as a guide only with regard to book content. Please note, such categorisation may not be universally upheld by all individuals and is open to interpretation across different readership demographics.

"Grandad's Army" contains real life stories, humour, bad language, romance and violence.

All rights reserved. No part of this book may be used or reproduced or transmitted in any manner whatsoever without written permission of Nemesis Publishing, except for brief quotations used for or within critical articles and reviews. For further information or enquiries, please contact enquiries@nemesispublishing.co.uk.

PRINTED AND BOUND IN THE UK

PUBLISHED BY NEMESIS PUBLISHING LIMITED

www.nemesispublishing.co.uk

Cover art by Claire-Louise Clements. Photos courtesy of Peter and Jean Flint

ISBN: 978-1-909251-22-9

DEDICATION

I WOULD LIKE TO DEDICATE THIS BOOK TO ALL THOSE MEN AND WOMEN OF EVERY RACE, COLOUR OR CREED WHO OVER THE CENTURIES LOST THEIR YOUTH... THEIR LIVES... THEIR LIMBS... THEIR SANITY IN WHAT WERE, FOR THE MOST PART, FUTILE, USELESS, STUPID WARS. MOST OF THESE FOLK WERE, LIKE ME, NOT HEROES BUT FOR A VARIETY OF MOTIVATIONS WERE DRAWN INTO HUMANITY'S ENDLESS INSANITY OF TRIBALISM AND CONFLICT...

Peter Flint.

Grandad's Army

Contains strong language, violence,
sex and scenes of nudity!

THE SENTINEL

He stands alone in the empty blackness of the night
Trying to remain alert... trying not to fall asleep
The terrifying march of Time's eternal turning
Keeping pace with the nervous pounding of his heart
His mind drifts between memories of peace... home
And the terrors concealed in the all-embracing dark
Fear... boredom... both battle for control of his brain
Ahead in the stygian gloom, lurks the unknown enemy
Sinister creatures in thrall to all that is ultimately evil?
Or... trembling, frightened, bewildered lads like himself
Innocents pitched into the blood-soaked wasteland of war...
As the endless seconds slip silently to oblivion,
He thinks enviously of exhausted comrades sleeping
The comforting warmth of blankets and mugs of tea,
The far-off familiarity of well-loved friends and family...
At last, the sky begins to doff its cloak of gloom
Heralding the dawn...the welcome ending of his watch
Or the menacing advance of foreign foemen
Seeking the destruction of his young life's promise...

Peter Flint
July 2013

Report Document #001

BIGGLES FLIES OPEN

Few people realise that spots, pustules, zits robbed this nation of potentially one of its ace fighter pilots. The buff envelope containing a terse letter inviting me to quit the tedium of telephone accounting and present myself for medical examination at the Drill Hall in Derby beckoned me to the wild, blue yonder.

Armed with a more than presentable clutch of 'O-Levels'... that's GCSE's to you modern folk... and seven years of rigorous cross-country training, my progression to the pinning on of my 'wings' by Group-Captain Douglas Bader, or Rockfist Rogan, was a mere formality.

The written examination was just a doddle. The standard goolie-grabbing, coughing and whispering proved to be nothing more than an embarrassment. I approached the recruiting-officer's interview with equanimity if not cast-iron confidence...

"I'm sorry old chap, we can't take you in the R.A.F.," said the officer, glancing briefly at my application-form.

My heroic, aeronautical ambitions plummeted, engine screaming, to smash behind a convenient hill.

Peter Flint

"Why?" I heard myself croak.

"Well laddie, your medical examination shows you are F2... not up to R.A.F. standards I'm afraid..."

The years of pounding dark winter streets and muddy fields had at least given me some confidence in my own fitness. F2 sounded like cancer. I could not suppress the thought that, as in the case of a couple of my contemporary sporting heroes... ('no name no pack-drill' to quote a saying which would later become familiar...) F2 might mean 'Flat Feet...Two' and I might be excused the whole ridiculous business. After all, as a child, I had worn built-up shoes, leg-irons and had endured electric-shock treatment to prevent my developing fallen-arches and/or flat feet! However, this was 1952 B.C...

Before Clearasil!

Through a mist of disappointment and outright disbelief I heard him say, "You see, unfortunately the Medical Officer diagnosed you as having...acne!"

Although I was not one of those youths whose faces resembled a sunburnt Christmas pudding or the surface of the planet Mars, you did not have to tell me anything about the teenagers' terror... the plague of puberty... Acne! At the same time my eyes were drawn magnetically to breasts, bottoms, thighs, calves and my brains dropped between my legs, my face sprouted colonies of small, white, mattery mushrooms. Various ointments, oils, creams, steaming, squeezing... all only succeeded in increasing the crop. At the same time it decreased by a considerably higher factor my debatable sex-appeal and my fragile self-confidence. Now it seems my dermatological eruptions were to deny me my destiny... my rightful place with... 'The Few'!

"But...how...," I stammered, "does acne prevent me serving in the Royal Air Force?"

I expected some quasi-medical explanation along the lines that night sorties over enemy territory would be out as the zits would glow in the dark and reveal my position to Johnny Foreigner's air-defences. Sadly, the answer was more prosaic.

"We wouldn't be able to post you to a station in the Far East, you see. Climate and all that, you know... hot... sticky... not suitable for someone with your condition... sorry old chap..."

"Er...what happens now then?" I croaked.

The officer's face took on the expression of a used-car salesman. "Well, you could sign on with us in the R.A.F. you know. Three years... seven years... twelve years... good career... great opportunities in the R.A.F. for a bright young chap like yourself..."

"But...er...what you said...er...my...er...condition...?"

"The acne? Oh I daresay with a regular diet, lots of fresh air and exercise, no doubt it will clear up all in its own good time..."

Peter Flint

"If I don't sign on...what's the alternative?" I asked. Although naïve, I had already formed a rough idea of the answer...

"Well...it's a clear choice...either you sign on in the R.A.F. for a minimum of three years or I'm afraid it's downstairs to the Army..."

Although my generation of eighteen year olds expected our call-up papers for National Service in somewhat the same state of mind as youths in other cultures must have anticipated the ritual scars and the ceremonial whipping off of their foreskins, I feel sure that it was with a similar degree of enthusiasm.

So I went downstairs to the Army! I'm sure you are desperate to know what happened about the zits... I was posted to Japan which, as even those who got a despairing 'E minus' in Geography must know, is about as far East as you can go without coming back!

I suppose in this age of 'Celebrity', most folk would be thrilled and honoured to have an all-singing, all-dancing, ticker-tape acknowledgement from their home town. As I boarded the bus from Ilkeston market place, clutching the cardboard suitcase containing my regulation 'razor, comb and lather-brush', the Town Hall was ablaze with lights. The town was 'en fete' as I left but this was not a 'rally of relief' because I was leaving, it was merely a symbolic coincidence as the bus bore me away for two memorable years.

Grandad's Army

I arrived at the Royal Berkshire Regiment barracks in Reading on a dark, foggy evening in early October. Today, folk hop in their cars and drive a hundred miles or more to visit family and friends or to see a show. However this was almost the first time I'd travelled more than twenty miles away from home and certainly my first trip alone. I have old photographs of my only other voyage... a family holiday... a week at Blackpool. My only memory of this great childhood adventure is sitting, feeling very sick in a bilious-green tiled toilet which was easily the size of the Millennium Dome!

As I write, the picture of the barracks, the parade square and the mess-hall come stealing back, but a few things stand out above the rest... After being shown to the Spartan barrack-block which was to be our home for the next ten terrible weeks, we were pointed in the direction of the mess-hall to sample the delights of our first army meal.

The mess-hall was a huge, gloomy hangar of a place lit by green-shaded, dirty bulbs in its forward half... the rest being in miserable, ominous shadow. Scatters of long trestle-tables and battered metal chairs stretched endlessly into the gloom. A few 'real' soldiers were eating at one of these tables. They looked at our D.A haircuts - this scraped-back style favoured by the American recording artists' of the 50's and 60's - supposedly called so as an abbreviation of "District Attorney". The hair was scraped and greased so that the ends met at the back of the head in a line which was mockingly said to resemble a duck's nether regions... we lived in a much gentler age! They indicated our flowered shirts, string ties and 'brothel-creepers' shoes - usually in coloured suede, with a thick sponge sole - with expressions of mingled contempt, pity and hilarity.

I heard the story of the first army meal of a sprog such as myself where he complained, "Look, I've only got five peas!"

Whereupon, the cook said, "Fuck me, you've got one too many!" He then ceremoniously took one back!

My own first meal was memorable but decidedly unfunny being a harbinger of things to come. Two bored army cooks in greasy, dirty whites; their berets moulded to their skulls in the non-regulation style of those privileged members of the army on whom even N.C.O.s relied for favours; dipped long aluminium spoons into several large metal trays. The surfaces of these containers were opaque with an iridescent scum and their edges frosted thickly with congealed grease. Fish... cold, blue and unappetising like pieces of a decomposing corpse floated in a pool of globular water. Chips pallid and fatty, soaked up the liquid ooze while the peas each collected its own rainbow-coloured halo.

Within a few weeks I would have eaten this filthy sludge... not eagerly it's true but by then my civilian fastidiousness had virtually disappeared, dissipated by familiarity and, of course, hunger. On that first night though, feeling near to tears, I gulped down one or two soggy chips, then confined the remainder to its rightful resting-place... the swill-bin!

I recall the anguish I felt as the D.A. haircut; on which my barber and I had, over the previous several months, lavished labour and love into in the erroneous belief that its 'slimmed-down' form would literally pass muster; went under the merciless scissors. I will not bore you with further details of army-style haircuts, where this new and more unforgiving barber had to be bribed one shilling, or five pence to you modern folk, just to prevent him from running the shears over the recruit's scalp. Nor will I recount the issuing of our kit, save to mention the enormous berets, like giant woolly bin-lids, the stiff, iron-hard, pimply boots or the 'drawers-cellular'... Calvin Klein they were not... each pair had been designed to accommodate at least one platoon of infantry! I was one of the very few who accepted the hairy, knee-length long-johns... perhaps, even at that early stage in army life; I was astounded at being given a choice. As winter draws on I soon had my issue winter drawers on... by god they were itchy but at least they kept you warm down under... an over-riding consideration as I soon discovered.

The item of kit which secretly we most desired was the uniform, though it was not long before I couldn't wait to put on my brown, gabardine slacks and two-tone chocolate and cream shirt with the elongated pointed collar.

Peter Flint

The uniforms were woven from material created by mating a cardboard box with the woolly, fibrous matting then used as under-felt for carpets… if you still can't picture it, think brown fibre-glass! The sergeant who had already bellowed and humiliated us into a state of manic apprehension, then further added to our terror by informing us that we were to appear on parade the next morning with our uniforms PRESSED!

"Tomorrow morning at 08:00 hours you will appear on parade in your second-best B.D." Incidentally, that's the abbreviation of 'battle-dress' for you cissy civvies. "Your trousers will be neat and pressed into creases on which you will have to avoid cutting your nancy-boy little fingers. The B.D. blouse will also be neat and pressed… two parallel pleats vertically down each sleeve… three inches apart… NOT two inches nor four inches but THREE inches apart. The three pleats in the back of your B.D. blouse will be pressed to form parallel creases… three inches, six inches and nine inches…"

Most of us had mothers… by this time we were sure that none of the N.C.O.s had fathers… and mothers had always ironed our shirts, trousers and in the case of the posh lads, possibly their socks. True, we had all seen irons… I remember my Mum heating up the flat-irons in turn on the ledge in front of the fire and the spit sizzling on their smooth surfaces as she tested the heat. None of we lads had actually USED an iron and certainly had not the skill to produce creases… in parallel… three inches apart and ditto nine inches apart… in material resembling khaki roof-insulation!

Our suspicions that Vlad the Impaler had been reincarnated, given a red sash, three dazzling chevrons and a uniform with creases you could use to shave, filled us with a sense of panic.

We flocked like lemmings to a bare room containing two scrubbed tables draped with scorched, army blankets and one superannuated iron which was more dangerous to the British Army than Rommel's panzers!

One iron… seventy men! Strong men wept… weaklings fought… silken-tongued con-men bribed and wheedled. Sleep became a mirage… an irrelevance. Shortly after the clear notes of reveille sliced through the six a.m. icy darkness, ranks of battledress-blouses… and their bleary-eyed wearers… waited with something approaching the required configuration.

This was our initiation into the old army maxim which we quickly took to our hearts… 'Bullshit Baffles Brains'. 'Bull' combined with the brainwashing techniques utilised by all repressive regimes right up to the present day in Guantanamo Bay. Poor food, lack of sleep, frequent and incomprehensible commands, fear of punishments, unspecified, threats, shouting, ridicule and abuse are the army's methods of turning wayward-thinking, opinionated individuals into a disciplined, compliant mass.

Peter Flint

A barrack-room is effectively the same as a hospital ward in its general appearance but whereas the latter's god is hygiene, the former's is bullshit. Imagine a cold, dark barn of a room. Moans, whimpers, snorts and sobs form a counterpoint to stentorian breathing, creaks of bedsprings and agonising snores. It is the stygian twitching of the first circle of hell. Suddenly... the clear, piercing notes of a bugle... a light is snapped on and a gleaming, razor-creased, khaki-clad marionette strides thunderously between the huddled mounds of bedding, slashing the air with a polished pace-stick and shouting, "Wakey, wakey... you horrible little men! Hands off cocks... on socks!"

Groaning and shivering, pallid limbs emerge from warm, scented dreams to a harsh reality. Figures scuttle in the semi-darkness to splash and scrape their tingling flesh with needle-cold water. Twenty-four men... two washbasins... somehow it is done and the morning bull begins...

First... the locker. Shirts, vests, socks must be folded with squares of cardboard inside them to present a neat, 'licourice-allsort' elevation to the day's inspecting officer. Next... the bed. This must be stripped... the bottom blanket pulled drum-taut. The two grey blankets folded square and the green, top blanket pulled tightly round them so that they looked like a slice of twenty-year-old Battenberg Cake.

One's individual bed-space made ready... the communal effort began. The ashes were swept from around the enormous, but totally inefficient, iron stove. The recruits would then polish its surface until it gleamed. Meanwhile, once the floor had been swept, others toiled with their buffers and polish. Polish was spread on the deal planking and battered to a dull shine by the buffers... heavy metal pads wrapped in dusters, hinged to stout, six-foot, wooden handles. The technique was to swing the buffer so that it slid across the floor to the extent of its six-foot handle then, with a wristy-snap, the motion was reversed and the weighted pad hurtled six feet in the opposite direction. Finally a team of three or four would drag another member of their group around the floor on an old, folded blanket thus bringing the rough planks to something approaching a 'Come Dancing' shine.

Time was pressing... in minutes the company sergeant would appear and announce the 'second-coming'. This was usually some fresh-faced, erstwhile public-school boy with a plummy voice and a super-inflated ego. A rope was produced... no, we had not been panicked into the final solution... yet! This rope was stretched from one end of the room to the other. It was then used to perfectly align the ranks of beds, boots - studs uppermost and polished - mess-tins, knife, fork, spoon... clean spare bootlaces rolled, bedding as described and lockers. All that remained was to await the cry, "Barrack-room! Barrack-room...' shun! Barrack-room ready for inspection...sah!"

Eyes fixed to the front, necks clamped like early photographers' models, the ranks of rigid soldiery stood awaiting the moment when the sergeant's weather-beaten face would come into vision closely followed by a blond-haired, pink popinjay in immaculate dress-khaki and gleaming Sam-Brown belt. As if lifting a piece of festering garbage, he would broddle in the squaddie's meticulously laid out kit with a hand-stitched, leather swagger-stick and whinny, "Look at this s'arnt-major... this kit's filthy! It's disgusting! Slack work! Slack work private! A disgrace! Take his name s'arnt-major!"

The unfortunate miscreant would be impaled by the gaze of a khaki-clad giant, his chest filled with a rainbow splash of medal ribbons, who would stare in mock, outraged disbelief at a microscopic speck of blanco on a sparkling, brass clip or buckle. With gritted teeth, he would enter the wretch's name in his black note-book.

The first night I became 'a soldier' the lights were snapped out at exactly half past ten and I lay gazing at the lighter rectangles of the windows opposite, trying to come to terms with the events of the day and incessant scratchy-itch of the coarse blankets under which I was failing to sleep. Gradually I became aware of sniffles, whimpering and muffled sobs from the darkness and realised that my own feelings of being snatched from real life into a chaotic half exciting, half scary hell was shared by most of the boys thinking of family and home in the inhospitable shadows.

I made a vow... oft repeated in the months and years to come even unto this year's arctic winter... that if I got out of the army alive and with my assets unfrozen, I would never be cold again! I do not have the encyclopaedic power of recall like some writers who can tell you what the weather was like and how many currants there were in the slice of cake they had on their sixth birthday! Sadly, I now have some difficulty recalling what I did yesterday so I would just be indulging my imagination if I gave descriptions of icicles three feet long and snow piled to the rooftops that winter but Christ it was cold!

The parade square fronting the barrack-blocks was thick with sparkling, white frost; the branches of the trees stood black against a sky as scrubbed and bleak as the sergeant-major's heart. The frozen stillness rang with a bugle's note and spewing from the shadowy doorways of the barracks, frantic and clattering, came we recruits. Quickly we shuffled into ranks, each trying desperately to remember the basic elements of drill which had, by dint of threats, screams and bitter mockery, been etched indelibly on our memories.

That morning a new refinement of torture and humiliation was added which was to be repeated frequently and regularly for the next ten weeks… 'pokey drill'! For several minutes we stood; our fingers and toes beginning to sting and then burn in the cold, morning air. We felt the grip on our unfamiliar rifles becoming tighter but less confident as our finger-ends tingled. The officer in charge of the parade would then march onto the parade-square followed by the N.C.O.s from each company who would stamp their way like automatons to take up position; each with his own group of shivering squaddies. The officer would call out a command and the drill would be demonstrated by the N.C.O.s... punctuating their ritual with rhythmic stamping and bellowing counts of, "Lift... one, two! Out one, two! Hold it! Hold it!"

With varying degrees of success, the hapless recruits would try to imitate the effortless performance of the sergeants and corporals.

A Lee-Enfield 303, with sling, weighs just over nine pounds... not particularly heavy. Not particularly heavy until it is held at arm's-length straight out in front of your face in frost-numbed fingers as the agonising seconds tick away and the air echoes with a sea-gull screech of commands, exhortations and insults...

"Hold it! Hold it! Keep it straight!"

"What are you? A nancy-boy? Pretend it's your handbag you're holding!"

"Don't let it drop! You've been playing with yourself too much... haven't you... you 'orrible little man?"

"Sweet Jesus! God help us if you ever get near the enemy! P'raps he'll piss himself laughing at you Mummy's boys and you'll be able to surprise him!"

By this time, except for the lads from the fields and the pits, whose rigid arms were rock-steady, ours were shaking as if we had fever… our breath was forced in gasps through teeth clenched tight with effort.

At last the blessed relief would come!

"Rifles… rifles… rest… wait for it… wait for it! Squad! Squad… rest! Two… three… down… two… three… stand at ease!"

Chests heaving; arms stabbing with pain, we would pause until yet another fiendish, muscle-wrenching contortion would be commanded. Strong men winced; weaklings cried; while most of us hung on and prayed for it to end… which, of course, it eventually did… until the next day!

'Pokey-drill' was designed to develop on scraggy, pimply youths, muscles like those of Arnold Swartznegger. However, examining my own biceps after several weeks of pumping rifle, I concluded that in this instance, it had failed. It did achieve something… it fully developed other aspects of the personality… We conceived a white-hot hatred of the N.C.O.s! We feared the 'fizzers' and 'jankers' with which we were constantly threatened. We both admired and envied the assurance… the robotic ease with which our tormenters performed the excruciating or intricate tasks they demanded of us. We coveted their shaven, knife-edged uniforms, dazzling brasses, starched shirts, gleaming boots and profane vocabulary. We cringed at our own ineptitude and listened in awe to bawdy tales of forbidden quarters of foreign cities, drunken inter-service battles in obscure pubs and bars or heart-rending tales of action and death. We hated them but wanted nothing more than to be like them.

Peter Flint

One way in which their superiority over us was demonstrated happened daily on the parade-square. Most of us had been walking unaided... more or less... for at least seventeen years. Now we discovered that our feet had only the most tenuous links with our brains. In those first few weeks we were to relearn the art of walking... we were to learn how to march!

The histrionics of foreign armies cause much hilarity in the British army... the exaggerated goose-stepping of soldiers in various totalitarian regimes was ridiculed and mocked, as was the 'John Wayne' semi-shuffle of our American allies. No... the only way to march was the British Way! As with everything in the Army, there were two ways of doing it... the 'easy way' and 'the hard way'. As the drill-sergeant never tired of telling us, "The easy way's not easy and the hard way's fucking hard!"

Thus it proved! To propel one human being across a space in a parody of a clockwork duck; legs jerking rhythmically and arms swinging in time; was difficult enough. Marching, like most automatic human activities from tying a shoelace to making love, is fairly straightforward until you start to think about it... plan your moves... analyse your technique. Then, your feet, fingers and other appendages become 'thumbs' and your stress levels soar. It is difficult to imagine the vast number of people on this Earth who regularly and naturally, swing one leg forward and the opposite arm backwards at the same time. It is as natural as breathing... that is until you start thinking about it!

In every platoon there were several squaddies; brows furrowed and sweat-beaded; who waddled across the square closely pursued by an irrational, blasphemous N.C.O. who, by the sheer volume of his obscenities, was endeavouring to sever the invisible cord which jerked forward their right leg as their right arm rose.

When you consider the problems involved in getting the rookies to move forward in more or less a straight line, just think of the logistics involved in stopping, turning, moving backwards or sideways and avoiding obstacles! Do not forget that these manoeuvres, difficult enough for individuals, were to be performed in perfect unison by ever and ever larger groups. As if this was not enough to make the stoutest heart quake, all these things had to be done in different 'gears'... standard pace... slow time... quick time and double time.

The days ticked by and recruits jerked robotically off in all directions. N.C.O.'s voices became hoarse and their vocabularies exhausted. The day of the passing-out parade at the end of the ten weeks' training loomed large. Then this stamping, shouting, gibbering rabble must sweep past the assembled dignitaries, heads high, shoulders back and highly-polished boots cracking on the tarmac in synchronised rhythmic harmony. Of course, it then had to be done... with rifles...! But that's another story!

My own personal taste of parade-ground discipline occurred when a gravel-voiced sergeant demanded my name and number. Naturally, as I answered, I turned my head to look at the questioner...

"Look to the front you evil, little man! Look to the front! Look to the front... don't look at me! Who do you think I am... fucking Betty Grable?"

Now, I had seen Betty Grable - the curvaceous, blonde American film-star - in several films. She had probably also featured in a few of my X-rated teenage fantasies. I knew her legs were reputed to be insured for a million dollars and it was worth every penny, so I was fairly certain this was indeed not the famous Hollywood siren.

I muttered, "No, sarn't..." and prayed for the ground to open.

Brought up with the expertise and heroics of the likes of John Wayne, Alan Ladd and Audie Murphy, we waited half-eagerly, half-fearfully for the day when the rifle, which had been nothing but a source of alternate agony and embarrassment, would reveal itself as a weapon of warriors.

Many were the rumours whispered across the ranks as we marched to the range to actually fire live ammunition. Some knew the chemical composition of the explosive charge... others told of the gruesome impact that the bullets had on human flesh and bone. Yet others sneered at the inferiority of the weapons of other armies while the timid muttered of burst eardrums from the discharge and shattered shoulders resulting from guns too loosely held while firing.

The firing-range was a small, former quarry alongside a row of dingy, terraced houses. A line of wooden targets - four or five in number - were set up some fifty or sixty yards away from the firing-point against the sheer wall of the gloomy pit. What resembled the miniaturised grandstand of a particularly unpopular football-club formed the firing-points where we were to fire first the rifle, then the bren-gun... an automatic, rapid-firing machine-gun.

In the raw cold of an October morning, we sat, huddled in groups behind the firing-points. The air sang with the reports of the firing and an acrid smell of cordite-smoke bit at our throats. Officers, hands clasped behind their backs, chatted casually while N.C.O.s darted back and forth organising the next firing party.

With my own previous experience of firearms being nothing more than shooting at tin cans with an air-rifle, I was somewhat apprehensive when I was called forward. I lay down in the approved configuration... one leg stretched straight behind my body... the other, also stretched, at an angle to give extra stability. I raised myself onto my elbows, resting my rifle on the wet sandbags in front of me.

"Safety-catch... off! Five rounds - in your own time, commence firing!"

I squinted nervously through the sights and, with lurid stories of burst eardrums and shattered shoulders, echoing through my head, I squeezed the trigger. The noise of the shot reverberated in my skull like a tuning fork and the bitter smell lingered in my nostrils. I had hugged the Lee-Enfield far more tightly than I'd ever dared embrace my latest girlfriend so my shoulder remained intact. I saw a wand with a white disk to indicate where the shot had hit, appear from somewhere beneath the target but I was too relieved and elated to care. Almost nonchalantly, I squeezed off the remaining four shots; gathered up the empty shell-cases and lay awaiting the command to rejoin my chattering comrades.

Later… much later… that day we were given our initiation on the 'Bren'… a powerful, automatic weapon with an incredibly rapid rate of fire and virtually no recoil. I could almost visualise myself as John Wayne as I pumped a hail of shots into the far wall of the quarry. To tell the truth, I never did achieve any great degree of accuracy with any of the weapons I fired in the army. The red flag… indicating a complete miss… flew more often than in a rally in Red Square when I was firing, but I did find the bren-gun the most reassuring weapon I used.

In view of what happened later that afternoon, perhaps my faith in the bren was misplaced. I had completed my turn at the firing-point and sat, cold and hungry, waiting to march back to the comparative comfort of the barracks.

A plump, affable, ginger-haired lad called Benson, who was a member of the Plymouth Brethren, was settling his more than ample form behind the nearest firing-point.

His hands were trembling as he pulled back the lever to cock the weapon. When the command, "Fire!" came, he squeezed the trigger but nothing happened! Time was getting on and the N.C.O.s were no doubt anxious to get this dubious charade over and get back to the mess for a few beers.

With ease born of practice, the sergeant dropped prone behind the gun; changed the gas-regulator and, after re-cocking the weapon, squeezed the trigger... again, nothing happened! Cursing fluently, the sergeant went behind the firing-point and returned with the spare barrel for the weapon. He expertly removed the malfunctioning barrel and clipped the spare barrel into place. He got to his feet and ordered Benson back into his firing position.

The command to "Fire!" was given... Benson squeezed the trigger... There was a tremendous 'bang' and a cloud of black smoke issued from the gun. Benson gave a cry of fear and pain - he sprang to his feet shaking, his hands clutching his face which was covered in an oily, black film.

Pandemonium ensued! First Benson was mobbed by officers and N.C.O.s who quickly ascertained that he was not seriously injured before turning their attention to the much more important consideration... the bren-gun! Apparently, the explosion had somehow damaged the barrel... locking it in place. One by one, several N.C.O.s tried to release this barrel. They first tried twisting it... pulling and tugging it without success. They then moved on to more drastic methods... kicking it with their steel-tipped boots and finally, when this failed, swinging at it with a pickaxe!

It was obvious to even we rookies that all was not well as the arrogant poise of our mentors visible crumbled into a sort of restrained panic. Eventually, we were fallen-in and marched back to the barracks, having been warned on hurt of considerable unspecified pain that we had seen NO-ONE kick or pick or otherwise maltreat the damaged weapon!

In that less politically-correct era, Benson - who had become something of a hero - had to endure endless jokes about Al Jolson... the American 'black-face' singer and star of the first talking picture 'The Jazz Singer'. He grew tired of requests to perform the show's hit song 'Mammy'. I don't think any of us, including Benson himself, realised what a close escape he must have had!

Needless to say, no-one even joked about the violent attempts to free the barrel. I heard later over the 'grape vine' that there had been a formal enquiry into the incident which Benson had been called upon to attend. The outcome was that it had been some form of mechanical malfunction for which no-one could be blamed. I suspect that the sergeant, in a hurry to get the procedure finished, did not fasten the clip which secured the barrel into place, but no negligence was suspected. Like many closed communities, the army looks after its own!

As the weeks passed, the routines were established; mysteries explained and fears dissipated. We had built up camaraderie in the platoon forged in fear and toughened in tribulation. Our uniforms no longer resembled badly-tailored potato sacks; we knew which end of the rifle should be pointed at 'the enemy'... were he ever to appear... and the communication between our brains and our feet had been, more or less, reconnected. At last we were deemed fit to be viewed by tax-payers who were financing our expensive, if frequently incomprehensible, training.

We were allowed out into the town... 'The pictures', dances and girls, were uppermost in our thoughts - though not necessarily in that order! We were, however, not allowed to wear civvies for our first excursion into Reading. Secretly we would, I think, have been offended if we had been as the opportunity to flaunt our military bearing was not to be missed.

One of our number - a cheerful lad from the South East - was anxious to put on public display his boots! Most of us had spent endless weary hours with melted polish rubbed into the toecaps and heels of our orange-rind footwear with the handle of a knife heated in the stove. This technique eventually smoothed out the blebs and impregnated the leather with a thin layer of polish. By further eons of spitting and rubbing in tiny circles, a mirror-like shine was finally produced. Most of us had achieved a passable gleam but Don was determined to go one better.

Peter Flint

The corner bed in our barrack-room was occupied by a creature of myth and legend… a tanned, monkey-like creature whom we rookies regarded with bewildered reverence. Jackson was a regular soldier and he had seen service and done 'jankers' in far-flung places whose names we could not even pronounce. He addressed sergeants and other demi-gods with a familiarity bordering on insolence. Apparently he was without fear of retribution for Jackson was fireproof! He had only one week and the traditional 'early breakfast' to do before the twelve or more years of army service were completed and he metamorphosed into that most fabulous of all God's creatures… a civilian!

Jackson had days to go and what is more, he had 'the boots'! Cinderella would have been envious of Jackson's boots. Twelve years… fifteen years… twenty-one years… who knows how many ages of patient boning, rubbing, spitting and endless tiny circles of polishing had gone into producing these glass-slippers! They gleamed, they shone, like raindrops in a Disney cartoon - the reflection went down and down into their depth forever and Don desired them!

He had realised before the rest of us that come Saturday, Jackson would have no need of these marvels and he had already imagined the adulation he would receive as they formed the centre-piece of his daily kit layout. Don soon fell to talking to Jackson… chatting about his tours of duty, his promotions and almost drunken demotions. Finally, the deal was done! Jackson had one final guard-duty to do but he wanted to say farewell to his favourite pub in town. He had to hand into stores two pairs of boots... any two pairs of boots! Don agreed to do Jackson's final guard-duty and swap his lustreless footwear for these Roll-Royces of the cobbler's craft.

Jackson had gone to that magical land where bugles did not sound in the middle of the night... where folk piled coal on blazing fires and no-one yelled, screamed or questioned your sexuality. It was Saturday and our first outing since our incarceration. Don was lacing up HIS boots which shone in the sunlight with a dazzling radiance.

How magnificently we strode down the main street of Reading that November evening, our heels clacking on the pavements in glorious unison. 'Left wheel!'... Into Woolworth's to wile away the time until the cinema opened its doors. With a magnanimous gesture, I flung a shilling into the cap of two urchins who were barely distinguishable from the Guy they were tending. Then I realised... I'd given them a whole day's pay!

Woolworth's was crowded. People pushed and jostled... shopping-bags, elbows and feet were everywhere. It was with some relief that we regained the relative tranquillity of the high street.

Horror-stricken, we looked down at the devastation of Don's wondrous boots... they were ruined! Scrapes and scratches scarred their once-dazzling surface like wounds. Years and years of work had been gouged and gashed into a disaster! We realised at that moment that these were not boots for WEARING! These were show-boots… glass-case boots… inspection-boots!

"By the right…eyes…right!"

Not quite the guards, but with our heads high, boots striking the asphalt in resonant time, we swept past the saluting base. Our berets had, by dint of tugging and even being kicked around on the barrack-room floor, remoulded themselves to our shorn scalps. Our cap-badges; a traditional memento of the regiment's famous victory at the Battle of Brandy-Wine where apparently hundreds of British redcoats gallantly defeated a handful of badly-armed but deceitful Indians, (back in the days when we still owned America); sparkled a regulation inch above the left eye on the red patch of felt.

The khaki-clad tide surged to and fro across the square… turning… stopping… advancing… retreating as one man. Rifles leapt to shoulders or clacked smartly to Earth as if feather-light bayonets scraped from scabbards and clicked into place and the parade marched proudly off the square. We had done it! We had survived the ten weeks of marching, running, cleaning, polishing, ironing amid curses and tears! Tomorrow we were going home!

Uniform brushed and pressed into knife-edged creases… trousers weighted with lead slugs on a leather lace (an 'illegal' method to make them hang straight and show off the creases) smooth, pale shirt and non-regulation knitted tie; this made up my outfit. I sat in a corner seat, trying to look 'cool' but really a cauldron of anticipation.

"Going on leave then, lad?" asked the elderly man seated with his wife on the opposite side of the carriage.

"Yes," I smiled. "Just finished my ten-weeks' square-bashing... first time home for nearly three months."

"Do you like it in the army, then?" he asked.

I was tempted to tell the truth but he seemed a nice, old chap, so I compromised... "Aye... it's not bad... a bit different from civvy-street you know."

"Aye, lad, that's true," he said, his eyes clouding momentarily. "Still, it's a lot easier than when I did my bit... we didn't get issued with them there patent-leather boots."

"Patent-leather boots?"

"No, it were all dubbin and hard work when I were in the mob," he said, shaking his head.

I looked down at my 'patent-leather' boots and thought of the hours and hours of polishing... the gallons of spit and the million of tiny circles! I was tempted to argue but the train was slowing down for Nottingham station. I was home!

Peter Flint

JOHN WAYNE COULD DO IT BLINDFOLD...

Training was not confined to 'bull' and marching... after all, we were to be turned into killing-machines... pre-Ramboing Rambo. This process involved much crawling around on our bellies... I came to realise what Napoleon really meant when he said, "An army marches on its stomach!"

We were trained to help our comrades over high walls despite the fact that we could have much easier trotted round them. We swung on ropes over muddy ditches; ran perilously across slippery logs and screaming, we disembowelled with our bayonets harmless sacks filled with straw. I accomplished this task with great zest but had a sneaking suspicion that the world had few evil empires whose troops resembled Worzel Gummidge!

There were times when the winter of '52 was too foul even for we lowly life-forms to be outdoors. When the wind howled and the rain slashed down, occasionally we had weapon-training...

On one such occasion, we were gathered in an empty barrack-room and instructed on the dismantling and reassembling of the bren-gun. We laid the various parts of the gun, which ranged from the barrel - solid heavy metal and almost two feet long - to tiny delicate springs, carefully in order. Then, on command, we would be required to reassemble the weapon, load an empty magazine, cock the mechanism and squeeze the trigger. This operation, complex enough, was being timed by the weapons-training instructor and inevitably became a race of fumbling fingers with profane accompaniment.

When we had all had our turn, we were then required to go through the same procedure... blindfold! Now, brain-powerwise I am not in the same league as Einstein myself, but some of His Majesty's P.B.I. (Poor Bloody Infantry) were, frankly, as thick as the proverbial porcine excrement and the N.C.O.s delighted in baiting them.

Bragg was one such - a lad from some southern farming village. He had been so inept in his marching that the drill-sergeant had threatened to put a piece of hay in his left boot... a piece of straw in his right boot and yell, "Hay...straw...hay!" instead of "Left...right...left!"

Bragg had already made several nervous to dismantle and reassemble the gun all the time to a running commentary in which images of copulation and animal husbandry were imaginatively combined. With a scarf tied around his eyes, he was now trying to put the weapon back together.

He cursed and struggled... picking up various parts of the gun... feeling them pensively; then fitting them into position or laying them aside until required. Into this scene strolled our platoon commander... a twenty-two-year-old whiz kid who, having tired of drinking coffee and trying to read the clues in the 'Daily Mail' crossword, had sallied forth for a little peasant-baiting. He signalled us all to be silent and took out the canvas spare-parts wallet which accompanied all brens.

Bragg, nearly desperate, continued with his laborious fumbling and grunting but the weapon was, at last, beginning to return to its operational state. With a grin, the officer placed on the floor several small pieces of the gun which he had taken from the spare-parts wallet. Inevitably, Bragg's nervous fingers found these parts and unaccustomed shafts of thought bounced through his head. His brow furrowed like corrugated cardboard and a blank look of puzzlement went across his face as he tried to reconcile the part which he was holding with one he had not yet replaced. Growling with frustration he would put back on the floor the piece which he was... almost... certain he had already fitted. He would then pick up another piece only to be faced by the same dilemma.

After several more minutes of increasingly blind, frantic scrabbling and more overt profanity, the lieutenant decided to put him out of his misery. Very quietly, he placed near Brag's hand the spare barrel! When Bragg's fingers closed over this, even he could not doubt that this large, heavy, metal tube had been replaced.

Peter Flint

Tearing the scarf from around his eyes and, with a shout of, "You...fucking...cheating...fucking bastard!" he looked straight into the eyes of his platoon commander!

Bayonets fixed, the line of enemy infantrymen advanced menacingly towards me across the icy crust of No-Man's Land. True to their murderous intent, they would continue to walk steadily towards me until, some twenty or thirty yards from my position, they would scream and charge forward to stab, tear and mutilate. I had a little over a minute to put together my trusty bren-gun which had been broken down and lay in all its numerous constituent pieces on a spread ground-sheet.

"For Christ's sake Flint... get on with it!" yelled the tense voice of the sergeant.

With a banjai scream, I flung myself down... right in the middle of the said groundsheet! Bits of bren bounced and shot off in all directions! The implacable line of grey-clad figures came ever nearer. Beside me the sergeant groaned, cursed and called on his gods. Needless to say, the position was overrun and I, inevitably, was killed!

Of course, as the previous episode was only an exercise, my reincarnation was immediate, although, judging from the remarks of the sergeant, the dying bit might become the real thing if I ever did anything so fornicating stupid again!

At times I did shake off my fear of being non-conformist and try to use my brain and initiative. On one occasion we were at a map-reading lecture on grid-co-ordinates. This could have been pretty dreary stuff except that the instructor had drawn the grid over a large photograph of a young lady who was extremely well-endowed but somewhat inadequately clothed! Plotting the co-ordinates of some of her contours... not to mention her outstanding features came as no hardship to a roomful of active, healthy, young males. The instructor had just called upon us to pinpoint a region of her anatomy most of us had dreamt about but never visited, when the clang of the fire-bell rang out...

Grabbing my beret, I raced out of the building, leading the rest of the class by several paces. I saw a column of smoke rising from behind a row of huts. A spade was stuck into the earth near some rose bushes. I snatched it up as I ran, thinking it might be of some use to beat out the flames or throw sand over the flames or batter down the door of the room in which the attractive W.A.A.F. officer with the great legs would be trapped awaiting my heroic arrival...

A small, brown canister lay in the middle of a patch of grass... clouds of black smoke were pouring from it into the grey sky. I dug into the soil and was about to try to smother it with several well-aimed spadefuls of earth when a raucous, upper-class voice demanded, "I say, soldier... what the bloody hell do you think you're doing?"

Peter Flint

I sprang to attention as taught, my trusty spade in the regulation 'shoulder arms' position and bellowed into the upper branches of the tree before me; "I was attempting to put out the fire...sah!"

"You leave that bloody smoke-grenade alone, laddie! In fact, stay there and make sure that no other silly bugger like yourself puts it out before the camp fire-brigade arrives."

The vision of standing proud before the assembled ranks while the company commander pinned my sergeant's stripes to my sleeve and the attractive W.A.A.F. officer with the great legs sighed longingly and glanced invitingly in my direction, faded on the instant. I slumped over my borrowed spade until a panting gang arrived pushing a red-painted handcart laden with several scarlet sand buckets and proceeded to bury the canister... so much for initiative!

Fire to primitive man was a god... a preserver of life through the dark bitterness of Britain's winter. Few species more closely resemble primitive man than your average infantry platoon and for them too, fire is an element of veneration and desire.

Much of the time in the winter of '52 we were outdoors, weapon-training; marching; shooting and much of the time we were very cold indeed.

Our hut was furnished with a large, cylindrical stove with a six-inch cast-iron stove-pipe which disappeared through the corrugated roof. It had a small, hinged door at the bottom through which ash and clinker could be cleared and a circular plate at the top to enable fuel to be fed into its capacious interior. But… wait… there was a snag… there was no fuel!

Shadowy figures crept out into the crisp air of the December evening. Quickly they scurried to the chain-link enclosure of the camp fuel-store. One by one they scrambled over the fence and began searching for coal to fill the buckets which they had brought with them. This was not an easy task, for, to their dismay, the store was well-nigh empty. However, after almost an hour of picking and scraping punctuated by heart-pounding pauses when the guard patrol came round, they had filled their various receptacles and melted back into the gloom.

Earlier in the day we had made preparations that no brazing equipment would be needed for any brass monkeys which should seek refuge in our hut. Two of our lads had scaled the roof of the hut armed with a length of cord to the end of which was tied a large boulder. This was lowered down the chimney and swung vigorously from side to side dislodging the encrusted soot and thus ensuring a strong, clear draught.

After our evening meal, the ritual stove-lighting began and soon the sub-zero clamminess turned into a warm, cosy fug. When the bugle sounded for lights-out, the guardians of the flames piled the roaring giant with fuel to the brim… even sprinkling a layer of coal-dust on the very top into which the iron lid sank snugly tight.

With the blessed luxury of heat, we slept the sleep of the just. We were, to say the least, astonished when we learned the following morning that the fire-piquet had entered the hut during the early hours to find us all sleeping like babes. Their concern had been caused by a two-foot flame, like a jet's after-burner, which was roaring out of the chimney. When they came into the hut to check, they had been amazed to see the cast-iron stove literally transparent with white heat… it was lovely!

* * *

"What are your observations concerning the behaviour of the dog, Watson?" queried *Sherlock Holmes,* puffing meditatively upon his favourite Meerschaum.

"The dog, Holmes?"

"Yes, Watson," said the great detective, the well-known gleam coming into his eyes. "Many would say that the dog didn't exist!"

We acquired the 'phantom' dog… a large, friendly red-setter… as we were crossing the busy A.40 on stage one of a fifteen-mile route-march cum map-reading exercise. Despite our protestations and even curses of our group, the creature was evidently firmly convinced that we were his bestest friends and was determined to join the 'fun' of our little fifteen-mile 'walkies'. We were all concerned for the animal's safety. As I have said, it was a beautiful, pedigree setter, obviously well cared-for and the road, a major route to London, was busy even in those far-off, tranquil days.

We decided that; as the beast craved our company; he was evidently lost and in danger of rapidly becoming an even redder setter, so we would take it along. When - *if* - we got back to camp, we would ring the owners whose name was on the metal tag on its collar. They would be delighted at our generosity of spirit and initiative and probably reward us handsomely.

Sad to say, our map-reading was not of the best and numerous discussions, diversions and reversals of our route must have eventually pushed the poor beast's 'walkies' to twenty miles or thereabouts. We finally arrived back in camp around six o'clock, feet aching; muscles creaking; throats parched and stomachs empty. We immediately set off for the mess, leaving the dog locked safely in the hut.

After we had eaten, we phoned the owners, fully expecting to be commended for our consideration and resourcefulness only to receive a torrent of abuse for 'dogknapping' the family pet! Its instantaneous release was demanded upon pain of our being reported to the C.O.

Injustice scalded like vitriol as we smouldered our way back to the hut. Not only had we almost certainly saved the daft mutt from death or injury, we had all grown fond of it… it was an honorary member of the platoon. We would

Peter Flint

release it to find its way home... when we were good and ready!

As we re-entered the hut, the dog was still there but there was one notable absentee... David Kirkpatrick.

David should never have been in the army or anywhere near it. He was the archetypal school's Physics Master or absent-minded professor. Tall and thin, bespectacled and brainy, David was not cut out for the rigours of square-bashing, pokey-drill and fifteen mile plus route marches. At first, when he had not returned to his hut, there was some joking as to how he would miss the cordon-bleu cuisine in the mess-hall but none of us was unduly worried.

Only two hours later when darkness had fallen and there was still no sign of David, did we then become a bit concerned. We went out enquiring and searching around the camp and in the mess-hall but to no avail. No-one had seen him since mid-afternoon when he had pleaded blisters and fatigue and sat down to rest. Rumour had it that search parties of N.C.O.s and even officers were scouring the surrounding area in considerable disgust.

It was well into the evening when the door of the hut opened and David's gaunt, exhausted figure staggered in. Dropping his kit, he stumbled towards his bed-space, no doubt to collapse dead beat on his cot. Unfortunately for him, stretched out on the aforementioned bed in an attitude of utter comfort and relaxation was... a large red-setter!

"Get off! Get off my bloody bed!" croaked David, his voice raw with weariness and disbelief.

The barrack-room comedian took immediately David's condition and, sensing an opportunity for some fun, said in a voice honeyed with concern and bewilderment, "Your bed, Dave? There's nobody on your bed!" This I suppose was debatably true...

"Don't be funny, Chris... you can see it as plain as me... there's a big dog on my bed," David retorted.

Chris chuckled then roared with laughter. "A dog? What in here? Where on earth would we get a bloody dog? You're knackered... you must be seeing things Dave, my old son!"

David began to get angry and waving his bony arms around in agitation, he cried; "I'm not hallucinating. There's a dog on my bed... a big dog."

By now all the lads were tuned in to Chris's idea.

"Come off it, Dave! If we had a dog in here, the R.P.s would have our guts for garters. For god's sake Dave, sit down... you're knackered... you're imagining things."

A chorus of pseudo-sympathetic voices echoed this opinion and a look of self-doubt crept across David's weary face.

"What colour is it, Dave?" asked one of the lads, grinning.

"Here," called another, "I'll get rid of it for you, Dave."

Peter Flint

He sprang to his feet and strode towards David's bed. With an expression on his face of a total lack of conviction in what he was attempting, he ordered the dog to move itself. His performance of solicitous pantomime would have won him an Oscar but, to our great delight and with an aggrieved look, the dog climbed down from the bed and flopped right across the central gangway.

Still not sure whether he was being set up, or whether the exertions of the day were causing him to hallucinate, David dumped his kit and slumped onto the bed staring at the dog.

After a minute or so, he said, "There is a dog!"

Mock cries of, "Where, Dave?"..."What, another?"..."Where is it now, Dave?" rang across the room.

"You lot are pulling my piss," said David, whose use of even mild profanity betrayed his inner turmoil. "There IS a dog and what's more, I'll prove it to you. Ginger, you walk down the hut to the door and you'll be bound to step on the bloody thing."

With a shrug which was supposed to indicate that he would do as requested but only to humour the poor loony, but which really meant that the game was up... joke over. He was bound to cause some reaction from the dog which was sprawled across his path right across the centre aisle. Ginger set off towards the door; eyes fixed firmly ahead ostentatiously demonstrating that this ridiculous test was totally futile. All other eyes were fixed on him… and, of course… the dog!

It had been a good laugh but now we were going to have to admit to our teasing. Ginger's next step would either land right in the middle of the dog's back or he would have to step short. He lifted his foot… The dog politely got to its feet and slid noiselessly into the adjourning bed-space. Ginger continued his unbroken stride and turned at the door to face a now totally bewildered David.

It seemed that the gag could not continue for long but, having rested for a few minutes, David dragged himself to his feet and announced that he was going over to the mess-hall to see if there was any food left.

You can imagine the remarks which accompanied his departing figure. You can also imagine the speed and glee with which we released the dog into the night to seek its owner.

By the time David returned from his meal, the 'phantom' dog was gone as if it had really never existed…

Tough as the route-marches and map-reading exercises were, they were only preliminaries to the real business of the army… killing people! At the time of my National Service, there was no shortage of people to kill as the enemy numbered well over six hundred million! You've probably guessed already… the massed population of China were ranged against we defenders of freedom… and capitalism in support of the Orwellian communist regime in North Korea. Those of you who have watched the U.S. television series 'Mash' at any time will know considerably more about Korea than I do and I have actually been there!

There was a not-so-funny joke circulating at the time about a lad who was trying to 'work his ticket'... Avoid National Service altogether by pretending poor eyesight. After more or less persuading the Medical Officer that he had difficulty reading even the boldest, blackest letters on the test card, he was led by the doctor to the window...

"Can you see that gate down there?" asked the doctor.

Feeling that claiming not to be able to see two six-foot, red painted yard-gates might be a little extreme, the lad answered in the affirmative.

"Would you see a Chinese if he came through those gates?"

"No sir!" snapped the lad.

"Would you see two Chinese?"

"'Fraid not, sir," said the lad.

"Ten?"

"No, sir."

"A hundred?"

"No, sir... sorry."

"A thousand?"

Thinking that he might be stretching belief a little too far, the young man answered that, well... yes... he might... if there were a thousand Chinese... just possibly be able to see them.

"Congratulations, son... you're in the army," cried the doctor. "If you could see a thousand Chinese, you'll be alright... we're sending you to Korea... there's fucking millions of the bastards out there!"

* * *

To kill someone it is necessary to get near enough to them to accurately aim a projectile at them or, alternatively, to stick something sharp and pointy into their vital organs. Needless to say, they will therefore do everything in their power to prevent you covering the intervening ground between their vitals and your sharp, pointy things. Therefore, you need to sneak up on them. While you are doing your sneaking, they are hurling in your direction a stream of metal, one small piece of which would remove the back of your skull and send it a considerable distance... not that you would know much about it. What you must do is to dissuade them from firing while you approach their position. This is achieved... hopefully... by the simple method of firing at them. There... easy... isn't it?

Peter Flint

The army have worked out a system to cover these circumstances. Each infantry platoon consists of two groups... a rifle group and a bren group. When a platoon comes under fire they fall on their faces... well, you would... wouldn't you? Falling on your face is quicker and, in the circumstances, probably considerable less messy than falling backwards!

Acting under orders, one group fires at the enemy, hopefully causing him to duck while the other group race forward to the next piece of cover from where *they* then fire while the first group race forward. Adopting this leap-frogging technique, the platoon is supposed to get near enough to the enemy to do them permanent damage.

The moorland was typical of its kind... rough hummocks of tussocky grass like whipcord, clumps of heather and tortured, misshapen, disillusioned bushes probably wishing that the birds had shat their seeds into some more hospitable environment.

We were practising the manoeuvre I have just described. One by one the platoons stumbled and staggered across the wasteland until given the command, "Under fire!" whereupon, the leap-frogging would commence.

For my sins I was our platoon's bren-gunner. Perhaps my superiors had realised that a rifle was completely ineffective in my hands unless I were able to get near enough to use the butt as a club or the rifle-sling as a garrotte. The bren weighs nineteen pounds; the spare-parts wallet eight or nine pounds; in each pouch at my waist I carried three full magazines… another twelve pounds. Add to this my helmet and pack and I was well-laden in contrast to my comrades who had only their rifles and packs to lug across the blasted heath.

"Under fire!" The sergeant-major's voice echoed across the moor and as one man, we hurled ourselves to the ground.

"Enemy… two hundred yards at two o'clock!" he cried. We strained to catch a glimpse of our phantom foe.

"Rifle-group… covering fire! Bren-group… on my command, behind that tree! Fire!"

Heaving the bren and all my other gear, I leapt to my feet and galloped, tripping and stumbling forward. Frantically my eyes searched for anything which could be remotely described as 'a tree'. I pounded onwards, some yards ahead of my comrades with the sergeant-major at my heels, whacking me repeatedly across my arse with a thunder-flash and screaming, "For fuck's sake man… run! Run!"

I ran… sweat poured out of me… my helmet rose and crashed down onto my head with every tortured step. The heavy pack smashed up and down and the bren clattered and banged against my shins.

I'm sure that, could it have spoken, the two-foot tall hawthorn twig would have been flattered beyond belief to have been called a tree… but, obviously to the sergeant-major, it qualified as a fully paid up member of arboreal society. It occurred to me that if this had been a real-life situation, something in the Canadian giant-redwood league would have been much more reassuring but I hurled myself alongside its slender form and cocked the bren.

"Fire at will!" roared the sergeant-major.

The imaginary *Will* had never done me any harm but 'orders is orders'... I pulled the trigger... nothing happened! I realised instantly that were this for real I had to get the bloody gun firing quickly or my companions would be pinned down by enemy fire, unable to advance.

I cocked the gun again... again I squeezed the trigger... again nothing! Okay first I.A... Immediate Action... change the gas-regulator. This I did... but still nothing! By this time my two mates, who made up the rest of the bren-group, arrived panting and gasping.

"Johnson!" bellowed the sergeant-major. "Lay down some rapid rifle fire while I see if I can get this fucking bren to work!"

"Flint, get out of the fucking way!" he screamed, giving me a look which implied that it was obviously my fault that a previously perfectly-functioning weapon now refused to spit forth its hail of death.

I rolled to one side to allow the senior N.C.O. to bring his years of experience to bear on the recalcitrant gun. Meanwhile, Johnson, who was to the right and slightly behind me, was obeying orders. Now, I cannot honestly say that I felt the wind of the bullet as it whistled past my right ear... however, I can truthfully say that the report was so close that my head rang like a bell. How near I came to becoming a casualty of the Korean War when I was still twelve thousand miles away from it, I'll never know. Still, as the old saying goes...

> 'A miss is as good as a mile!'

> ...amen to that!

* * *

I may now be going to ruin the whole story by admitting that I never got into combat. I never was able to test my rapidly evolving theory that my own team were more dangerous to my existence than the Chinese could ever be...

Imagine another bleak moorland landscape... the one you imagined before would do but, in fact, this one was different. It was high on a chalk ridge; the turf was close-cropped by sheep and feathery grasses were winnowed by the endless bitter wind.

Further killing practice... we were sitting in a circle waiting our turn to fire another of the infantry platoon's basic weapons... the two-inch mortar. There is nothing complicated or technical about the two-inch mortar. It is, as its name suggests, a metal pipe, two inches in diameter, closed at one end with a firing-pin... effectively the point of a nail protruding from the base-plate. To fire this weapon, one simply holds the pipe at an angle, the base-plate resting on the ground… and drops the mortar-shell tail-first down the pipe. In the tail of the mortar-bomb there is a propellant charge, rather like a shot-gun cartridge, which is detonated when the small percussion-cap hits the protruding nail… in other words the firing-pin as the bomb hits the bottom of the metal tube. All clear so far?

The mortar can fire several types of projectile in this manner. The two which we were waiting with quivering apathy to launch at yet another imaginary foe were a smoke-grenade and the star of the show… an H.E. (High Explosive) bomb. The smoke-grenade burst throwing out a billowing cloud of choking, black smoke through which our brave lads could advance unseen by the enemy. The fact that the resulting hacking coughs would pinpoint their positions to within an inch seems to have eluded both the inventor and the military high-command.

The second missile… the High Explosive… this could scatter small pieces of anyone near its point of impact over large areas of the battle-field. The H.E. was sent on its way in exactly the manner which I described except that, before the missile was slid into the tube, it was necessary to unscrew a sturdy metal cap from the business end. This exposed a burnished, copper dome whose delicate surface hid the detonator which set off the main, lethal charge. As the bomb hit the ground, the dome crumpled, compressing the detonator… and… BOOM!

Imagine a bleak moorland… oh, you've already done that! Sorry but without the technical data this story sort of lacks a point. One by one, we slid the bombs down the tube… watched them soar across the valley… saw the billowing, black smoke or the bright flash followed by the sharp crack of the explosion.

I suppose the first five… six… were moderately exciting… the next twenty or thirty had the stimulation value of a ten-year-old railway timetable!

'For Christ's sake drop the fucking bombs and let's get back to camp for a warm and a mug of hot tea' was the prevailing thought…

Luckily for us, our second-lieutenant who was supervising the drill, was not dreaming of a snifter with the chaps in the mess before dinner. As I have said, many of the British Army's infantry would have made an amoeba look intelligent. Such a one now shambled forward to hurl fire and destruction into the heavens…

Off went the smoke grenade in fine style. We glanced idly across and estimated how many more there were separating us from that stove and our mugs of tea. With horny, grubby hands the 'amoeba' unscrewed the green, metal cap on the H.E. grenade. He held it over the mouth of the tube and…

"Jesus Christ!"

The lieutenant's voice cracked as swiftly as his hand darted out to catch the tail-fin of the bomb as it began its slide towards the waiting firing-pin! Yes... that's right... you've worked it out! The fragile metal dome covering the explosives' detonator was going down the mortar tube first!

To quote the Duke of Wellington describing infantrymen of more than a century earlier, "I don't know what they'll do to the enemy... but, by God, they terrify me!" Right on your Dukeship... me too!

* * *

With days rather than weeks to go before we were to be launched against the might of Red China... looks lovely on a white table-cloth... Red China looks lovely on... never mind... With days to go before embarkation for Korea, we had become skilled in the use of a variety of weapons and moving quickly across rugged terrain to engage the enemy... or had we?

Our company lay concealed behind pine trees at the edge of a small wood. Each man was carrying a loaded rifle... ten rounds of gleaming death. In each platoon was a bren-gun which could spit out its magazine of thirty rounds in less time than it takes to tell.

Quietly each platoon of ten men moved through the trees until they emerged facing a gentle hillside. Hurling themselves to the ground they poured a merciless fire at the grey figures crouched in the bracken before them.

When the whole company of three platoons had reached the border of the wood and blasted away at the enemy, the officer in charge called, "Cease firing!"

Tingling with excitement, we moved across the shallow valley to discover what our barrage had done to the enemy. Twenty-seven magazines, each with ten rounds… three bren-guns… thirty rounds each… in total 360 bullets, had been aimed and fired. However, as we examined the plywood warriors who had been our targets, the verdict was that we might just have seriously wounded one man!

The steep slope of the hill stretched upwards seemingly forever. Panting, swearing, slipping and sliding we made our way towards the ridge, hauling on bushes, digging our fingers into tiny holes in the slippery turf. Eventually the slope became gentler and we were able to form up into some semblance of a line and move, rifles at the ready, towards the enemy trenches.

Some thirty yards from where the (theoretical) enemy were dug in the order was given to… "Charge!". Yelling like banshees, we hurled ourselves forward. My chest was pounding… sweat was pouring into my eyes but I managed to gallop clumsily across the open ground to throw myself into the nearest trench, stabbing viciously at an imaginary opponent before stumbling onwards some fifty yards to where we were to regroup.

We lay, gasping for breath and totally exhausted in a most unmilitary heap having overrun a line of empty trenches! My imagination ran riot… what if there had been men in those trenches? Nasty, little, slit-eyed men who had not clambered up a steep hill... not run across fifty yards of barren, open ground but had sat there... waiting? I realised that in the condition I was in when I had leapt into that trench, a Chinese baby could have swatted me with its rattle... I also realised that in a little over a month we would be in Korea!

* * *

By the way, did I mention? We did see the phantom dog again... all four hundred of us... it was like this...

The buzz of rumour went round the camp that the muster-parade that morning was to be something special. A local girl had been 'put in the club' as the expression of the time had it and she was coming to identify the 'father'!

Therefore, it was with mixed feelings of awe, envy and apprehension that we stood at attention that day. I would imagine that many, including myself, were matching our sexual aspirations and almost total lack of experience with this evil, shameless... heroic figure that had not only done it... but had proof!

'Four-hundred and twenty virgins...' (Well, I reckon most of us were), all stood gazing resolutely forward as the C.O. appeared with a young woman at his side. For all we knew, she could have been his daughter, brought to look at daddy's rough soldiery... if she was indeed the Colonel's daughter, our unknown cocksman was a double-dyed hero... or fool!

Four hundred(ish) minds with but a single thought... well, to be accurate, two single thoughts... 'Christ! What if she points to me?' and 'I wonder what it was like.'

For an endless couple of minutes, she gazed intently along the khaki-clad ranks; then she and the C.O. walked off. Did she identify her paramour in the lines of fresh faces in front of her? I will never know... nor, for that matter will you. All I do know is that, as her eyes ranged half-accusing... half embarrassed along our faces, the phantom dog ambled casually across the parade-ground behind her and the C.O. I could almost sense David Kirkpatrick itching to take that fatal step forward to vindicate himself... fortunately, he didn't!

Peter Flint

Grandad's Army

Report Document #003

MANOEUVRES IN THE DARK

Nowadays business executives are sent on self-awareness courses which include 'war-games'. They dress up in designer jump-suits and chase each other through the woods… I'm sure one becomes very self-aware in these circumstances! These characters do this sort arduous, dirty, pointless exercise for fun… we we did it because we were ordered to!

Just before we were due to sail for Korea, all the murderous techniques we had been taught were, theoretically, to be incorporated into a kind of dress-rehearsal lasting three days. My geography has never been particularly strong but this pantomime which was to involve more men than Cecil B. De Mille's films… guns, flares, tanks and other military hardware, took place on the South Downs near Swindon.

Because I was fleet of foot, completely useless with most types of weapons… or both… I was nominated as 'Company Runner'. This meant that it was my job to carry messages from my Company Commander to other officers on the battlefield. There was good news… not the messages that I had to carry… but related to this job. The good news was that the Company Runner might be required at a moment's notice and was therefore excused the back-breaking chores and mind-numbing exercises of the other infantrymen. The bad news was that, in a real battle, runners were the ones who had to sprint across No-Man's Land to relay some fatuous request from some upper-class twit who had never thought of using… the field telephone!

Further bad news was that, in order to make these manoeuvres more realistic… as if sleeping under a groundsheet on a dew-drenched hillside wasn't realistic enough… my Company Commander decided that he would have to send a message in the middle of the night!

After my eyes had become accustomed to the faint, far off gleam of the stars, I stumbled across the chalk hills, hopefully in the direction of Charlie Company's slit-trenches. I was cold… I had slept… if at all… fitfully on the hard, damp bosom of Mother Earth. My comrades were at least curled up under their groundsheets, swathed in as much spare clothing as could be worn under a greatcoat while I was stumbling and cursing through the star-glimmering blackness.

Suddenly, I saw the shadowy tumuli of a group of slit-trenches and moved forward. I was almost toppling into the nearest trench, when a sleepy, irritable voice growled, "Halt! Who goes there?"

The sentry sounded almost as enthusiastic about this charade as I was but I had the edge in irritability as I had floundered almost three quarters of a mile over the blasted heath.

"It's the fucking 35th Serbo-Croation Boy Scout Division moving through," I snarled.

"Oh… O.K. then mate," grunted the sentinel.

"Is this Charlie Company, mucker?" I asked.

"No, we're Dog Company… Charlie's over there… er… I think…" he said, moving sleepily back towards his trench.

I set off on my night time trek, once more thinking that, in a few more weeks, that bloke might be guarding me from the cunning infiltration of the evil, slant-eyed, yellow hordes…

As I have said, part of the job of being a Company Runner was that one did not have to deal with such menial, peasant chores as digging trenches. I had already had my fill of digging trenches (is that a contradiction in terms?) before I was selected for my human Pony Express duty…

My hoppoe and I were prodding away, sweatily but ineffectually and unenthusiastically, at a two-foot layer of chalk below which was another two-foot layer… of flint! The chalk was relatively easy to move with the infantryman's most efficient weapons… a pick and shovel! The flint, however, was a 'pig' to shift… being hard and loose, it was of no use hacking at it with a pick and virtually impossible to make any impression with a shovel.

Thus it was that we were scraping, swearing and prodding wearily at the shallow, three-foot deep depression we had managed to produce, when our Platoon Commander strolled over, presumably to admire the handiwork of his gallant lads. For some reason, he was unimpressed and remarked on this and other extraneous matters concerning our sexuality and genealogy. He then instructed us to, "Make the bloody thing deeper or when we get back to camp, you'll be in the Guard Room so fast your feet won't touch the floor!"... Or some similar traditional Army form of motivation and encouragement.

The injustice of this pompous, little prat who probably wouldn't know which way up to hold a shovel, telling us we were lazy, idle etc, etc. made us determined to take him at his word. Deeper was what he wanted and deeper was what he was going to get! We really made the chalk and the flint fly and burrowed like moles into the Downs.

A slit-trench is, as its name suggests, a slit cut into the earth to protect the soldier from enemy fire. Ideally it is about five feet deep and three feet wide... the front of the trench has a step about eighteen inches high upon which the soldier can stand, resting his elbows on the breastwork of earth thrown up whilst digging the trench. From this position he can fire upon the enemy while remaining fairly well protected. If the trench is to be occupied for any length of time, it is dug in an 'L' shape and one side of the 'L' roofed over and used as a sleeping place.

When the officer returned, he discovered that his orders had been obeyed... to the letter! We had gone down at least seven feet and whilst there was very little possibility of the enemy seeing us there was absolutely no chance of us seeing him! For some reason the lieutenant didn't seemed pleased with our efforts!

All around khaki-clad figures toiled with their picks and shovels while myself and a lance-corporal, who was the Company Runner of Dog Company, lolled around waiting for some vital message to be carried hither and yon. Basking in self-satisfaction... and idleness, we were blissfully unaware of the approach of one of the lesser gods... the Regimental Sergeant-Major! Unaware that is until a voice of thunder bellowed...

"Nah then! Nah then! What are you idle little men doing? Why are you not constructing a slit-trench?"

"We're Company Runners, S'arnt Major," replied the Lance-Jack. "We could be called to take a message at any minute..."

"Yes, and if this were a real war instead of an exercise you two bloody nancy-boys could be fucking shot at any minute... so get fucking digging!"

Sane men did not argue with the R.S.M. so we rapidly 'got fucking digging'. However, after ten minutes or so of sweaty labour, the R.S.M. and our enthusiasm had disappeared so we called a halt. We had produced a grave-like shallow pit about six feet long and a mere foot and

Peter Flint

a half deep. The R.S.M. did not return to monitor our progress. We were also kept moderately busy running messages around the various troop dispositions until darkness fell and we heard the bugle sound 'Lights Out!'

As there is little nightlife on the blasted heath except the creepy-crawly variety, the only thing to do was to get one's head down and sleep… a favourite army pastime known affectionately as 'Egyptian P.E.' Our shallow pit was ideal for lying at full stretch, a groundsheet beneath us and one on top to protect us from the wet and our heads resting comfortably at either end on the level sward.

I'm sure you will all be aware that psychologically, the best time to attack an enemy is at first light. To you folk who have never realised that before the sun comes peeping over your windowsill, there is an hour or so of dirty, depressing semi-darkness… this means about three-thirty a.m. At first light, so the army has it, the enemy are sleepy, lethargic, dispirited and vulnerable. Which genius sat scratching his head working that out we'll never know but he is undoubtedly correct so that is the time to hit the bad guys with everything you've got. The obvious counter to this 'he knows I'm knackered so he's going to attack' is 'he doesn't know that I know that he knows that I'm knackered so he's going to attack' so I'm going to get up especially bright and early and be ready for him!

As the sleepy sentries blinked to ascertain whether their eyes were playing tricks or the black silhouette had which they had been staring really hard for some time really was a tree, gradually from the blackness detail began to emerge the strident bugle blast of 'Stand To!' and hundreds of huddled figures cursed into wakefulness.

The Lance-Corporal and I, too, opened our eyes and blearily gazed at the grey sky rapidly lightening into full day. Fresh as a daisy, crisp, shaven and fully-dressed, the R.S.M. bore down upon our recumbent figures. Of course, all he could see were two apparently upright and alert heads protruding from either end of a slit-trench, covered with a groundsheet.

"Well done, lads," he growled. "That's right... up and at 'em! Come on, get that groundsheet stowed away now."

We were petrified. Seeing two heads, he had naturally assumed we were standing in a deep trench... not just lying in a shallow one! What would this demigod say when he discovered that his crack troops, eager, alert and on their toes were, in fact, prone and pissed-off?

I feel you, dear reader, are far too delicate and genteel to imagine the character-references we received and the torments which were to be inflicted upon us as, like two shy striptease artistes, we pulled away the waterproof to reveal our comfy... but all too shallow... hidey-hole. Suffice it to say that his language was... well... colourful! Fortunately for me, being a private soldier... there is nothing lower that squirms and wriggles on the entire face of God's good Earth... the full blast of his anger and contempt seared my N.C.O. companion.

* * *

Only once during my two years' National Service can I recall being physically afraid for my life. This happened while we were taking part in our final pre-Korea manoeuvres. I had been ordered in the middle of the night to take a message across open country... why plans and deployment could not be communicated during office hours I'll never know.

Once again, the small hours found me stumbling hopefully in the direction of the unit for whom the information was intended. Once again, I pondered the futile hours spent by super-intelligent boffins perfecting instant, reliable communication devices such as: radio, telephone... the penny-post. Once again, muggins was following his nose in the dark across open country.

The exercise in which we were taking part was designed to be as realistic, as authentic as possible... after all, the Red comrades in Korea were playing for real. Therefore, the powers that be were not only using we 'grunts' as the P.B.I. came to be called in Vietnam... which, by the way, was yet another costly war to stop the spread of the Red Menace in South East Asia... mechanical units, including tanks, were deployed.

Tanks are the gigantic, metal monsters which provoked peaceful German farmers to look at their wrecked fields and torn-up village streets and plan the Fourth Reich!

We had seen a few of these juggernauts parked... their arrogant pilots, with bizarrely moulded berets adorned with the lances, pennants and mottos of long-defunct squadrons of hussars. They regarded us with lofty disdain while we made supposedly funny remarks about sardines etc. We had not actually been involved with this arm of the services although, the merits of plate armour for hiding behind while moving forward or the perils of being in front of one of them while it was moving forward were much discussed.

I, you will recall, was plodding through the star-lit gloom thinking my own thoughts... warmth, bed, girls, civvy-street preferably all at the same time when out of the darkness rearing before me was... a tank!

I have read that when death is inevitable, your past life flashes before you. I must have led a very dreary, sheltered life for all that flashed through my mind was... "Jesus Christ! A fucking tank... I've had it!"

The huge mass clattered and rattled with a deafening noise but strangely it did not move!

When my heart had settled down to a mere machine-gun rattle, I crept forward, puzzled, to investigate. What I had taken for the threatening bulk of a tank about to crush me was an enormous elderberry bush. The terrifying

Peter Flint

clatter was made by hundreds and hundreds of roosting birds whose peaceful slumbers I had disturbed!

* * *

Because of my previous existence as a civil servant, I had been given a lowly clerical job in the Company Office. This was partly envied by my fellows as it kept me warm and not too overworked while they reluctantly did manly, soldierly things in mud, rain and wind. Thus, I was somewhat mystified and annoyed… though I decided not to mention this… when I was told to get my rifle and web-equipment and parade outside the guardroom with a motley band of drivers, clerks, cooks and other decidedly unmilitary personnel.

We were inspected; sneeringly issued with ten rounds of blank ammunition and marched out of camp along the road towards the open countryside. It was by now ten thirty at night, dark and threatening rain but by now we had come to expect the unexpected.

We marched several miles to where the road levelled off on the crest of the Downs and passed alongside a small copse. Here it was finally explained to us that we were to conceal ourselves. We were to impersonate the enemy and ambush the main body of our company which would be practising a night attack… what a jolly jape eh chaps?

Midnight came and went… one o'clock came and went… the promised rain came… and stayed! We crouched under the trees, peering into the blackness every minute expecting the stealthy skitter of an advancing scouting party or the fiendish yell as, having crept silent as wraiths to within a few paces, our comrades launched their attack.

Two o'clock and our clothes were almost as cold, damp and clammy inside our rain-streaked ponchos as our heads and feet were outside. Muttered questions and rumour flew back and forth…

"When the fuck are they going to come?"

"It's raining i'n't it? The poncy, fucking officers won't be coming out in the rain… will they?"

"Right… they'll have called it off…"

"Eh corp, do you reckon they've called it off, eh?"

"I'll bet they've fucking called it off and forgot to tell us… fucking typical that is!"

""Yeah, couldn't fucking organise a booze-up in a brewery… fucking army!"

"Shurrup… there's someone coming!"

True enough we could hear the tramp of marching feet coming towards us along the road… we were puzzled. As I have said, we were probably the least military group in the whole outfit… bad-eyes, piles, boils, flat-feet, excused boots. We would have made Scutari look like a health farm but we had assimilated sufficient combat lore to realise that you did not march in column of three into a surprise attack on a concealed enemy. Hence we were puzzled and bitterly disappointed desiring nothing more than to be taken prisoner… or even 'killed' so that we could get back to camp and bed for the precious few remaining night hours.

The shadowy outline of the marching column appeared over crest about a hundred yards away.

"Do we fire, corp'?"

"Can't be them… they wouldn't march straight down the middle of the fucking road, would they?"

"Who the fuck is it then?"

"It must be the fucking Green Howards coming back from a night march… their camp's about three miles down there."

The column swung past and the tramp of feet faded as they disappeared down the hill, leaving us fuming and frustrated at the thought of their luck in soon being snug abed.

Time crawled by. We became… if that were possible… colder. Rain trickled inside our ponchos and our boots. We had almost given up hope of being killed or captured when we again heard the sound of marching feet… from the other direction!

"I don't care who the fuck it is," cried the corporal, "Fucking fire!"

We, relieved to be doing something... *anything*... at last, blazed away with our blank rounds and hurled thunder-flashes towards the road.

Yells and barked orders mingled with the crackle of rifle fire and the crack of thunder-flashes as dark figures charged into the wood.

"Put your hands behind your fucking head... you're captured," said a wet, miserable-looking squaddie, pointing his rifle at me as I stood against my sheltering tree.

"Thank Christ for small mercies!" I said, raising my arms above my head.

In an all-too-rare humanitarian gesture, urns of scalding hot tea had been laid on in the mess as we returned, tired, drenched and depressed. As I was sipping the reviving liquid from my mess-tin, a superior being deigned to address me...

"Why the bleddy hell didn't you men fire when you first saw us coming dine the road? Christ, what an absolute shier!"

"Excuse me, sir, but when do I collect my Victoria Cross? Twelve men, with rifles attacking a heavily-armed column marching... yes... *marching*... down the middle of the road..."

"That's enough of that, soldier," he barked.

Peter Flint

You have to understand… two things you were never allowed to do in the army… argue with a superior officer… or think!

Report Document #004

TOMMY CRUISE

Docklands has acquired a certain cachet with the development of high-cost yuppy units on the Thames but I cannot recommend a five-day holiday on Southampton Docks. Our enforced holiday, complete with organised aerobics and other sporting activities made the front pages of the national press....

'PRISONERS ON THE DOCKS'

Or some similar headline bemoaned the treatment of 'Our gallant lads off to defend the principles of democracy and freedom' and all the rest of the platitudinous nationalistic claptrap which fills the front pages even today. The generator on the troopship, which was to carry our battalion of the Royal Warwickshire Regiment to replace the Durham Light Infantry in Korea, was broke and the ship could not sail.

Naturally, a few days extra in Blighty exploring the fleshpots of Southampton appealed to us no end. We were disappointed and angry when we learned that there were to be no shore-leave passes issued. We were even further incensed when told that a programme of marches, rifle-drill, weapons training and P.E. had been organised to keep us busy on the docks until the boat had been repaired and could sail. It was only later that I realised why we were to be so confined… many of the lads were less conformist than I was and once ashore had no intention of returning aboard. Fearing considerable numbers going A.W.O.L., the Battalion Commander had determined to keep us occupied on the docks until the repairs were completed.

Someone had got to a telephone… (Nowadays every squaddie would have at least three mobiles!) and informed the press that 'our brave boys' were being held on the quayside and we hit the headlines… and so the excrement impacted with the revolving blades!

For the three days before the ship eventually left harbour, we were allowed into town. I would like to report a drama, a romance, a debauch but… sorry Southampton… I can remember nothing at all save that the 'Orwell' left minus seven squaddies!

* * *

Few will, I am sure, recall the stalemate reached in the Korean War and the 'on-off' protracted peace talks at Pan Mun Jong. A friend of mine swears that the troopship carrying the Essex Regiment which left some two weeks ahead of us, actually leapt out of the water when the news came that the uneasy truce had actually been signed. Relief was an understatement when, three days before our departure, the war ended. We remained, however, apprehensive, as the treaty seemed; even to our naïve, apolitical, eighteen-year-old minds; a fragile, cobbled-together affair which might break down at any moment. Also, we had heard of the ferocity of the bitter Korean winter and the idea of spending it in slit-trenches even without the threat of attack and death was frightening in itself.

My only previous experience of the sea had been a week's holiday at Blackpool when I was three years old. Faded family snapshots show me happily filling a bucket with sand and nervously riding on a donkey but of these pleasant moments I have absolutely no recall. My mother often told me that I was, in fact, sick all the week of the holiday. That too remains a total blank. I can remember only one thing... sitting feeling lonely and frightened in a toilet which was walled with bilious, green tiles and was easily the size of the Millennium Dome!

You can imagine my feelings when I first saw the waves lapping at the quayside and the towering white bulk of the troopship.

The sea and ships were only seen in films where satin-clad, elegant ladies with tantalising scarlet cupid's-bow mouths gazed dreamily across the shimmering, moonlit waves awaiting the fortuitous arrival of a slim, dinner-suited gallant with sleek, gleaming hair and pencil moustache...

The romance of a thousand movies ill-prepared me for the grim reality...

Peter Flint

Into a vast, shadowy, metal cavern lined with endless ranks of three-tier bunks, we excitedly clattered down steep stairs. Four hundred young men, laughing and chattering, hurled their kitbags and webbing onto a bunk - establishing their territorial rights for the next five weeks. We lined up and were issued with a bedroll... this was a canvas strip, six feet long with brass eyelets along each side. I originally thought of Drake swinging in his hammock 'sleeping down below' but quickly realised that he would indeed have slept 'down below' as he would have inevitably fallen onto the deck had he attempted to use the narrow canvas strip as hammock. Inside the canvas strip was a blanket and a pillow... and that was that!

As the ship's siren blared we felt the first tremors and, almost unbelievably, the gap between the dock and the towering side of the ship widened... the exotic image returned. I stood with two companions and marvelled as the land dwindled and the churning wake stretched away into the distance. We talked of nothing but the sea the ship and the voyage. We were bursting with excitement... today's world of instant travel; cars; boats; planes; was, at that time, an impossible dream...

Oh if the idea of the voyage was a dream, then the Bay of Biscay was a nightmare! Four hundred men packed tightly into a confined space; the noise, the smell, the lack of privacy sent us scurrying on deck or to the canteen. Then came the seasickness! The deck, the latrines, the washrooms were swilling in vomit as four hundred lads;

many who, like me, had never seen the sea let alone sailed on it; came to terms with an alien element. We spewed and retched, collapsing onto our bunks only for the evil stench to send us racing for the open air.

It was several days before our insides settled and the routine of life aboard began to establish itself. To me it was magic... the sparkling, endless blue of the sea; porpoises leaping in the bow-wave of the ship as it cut through the water. Once someone said he had spotted whales spouting but I strained my eyes to no avail. On other days the sea rose in huge slopes higher than the boat and flying-fish leapt like silver arrows from their sides.

I do not know what I expected from my first glimpse of a foreign land. Actually it was a white-painted, brick building of no particular interest but the palm trees growing in front of it made it the setting of a thousand imaginings.

Gradually we adjusted to life aboard ship. We were occupied with the usual routines cleaning brasses, P.E., weapons training and lectures. It was this latter which I have regretted all my life!

I have always longed to be a piratical free-spirit but natural cowardice and an over-active imagination made me a craven conformist. I noticed, however, that while my mates and I were running round the deck; breaking down and reassembling all manner of weapons, squirming at gruesome film-shows depicting what happened to unwary willies in foreign places; many people seemed to spend all their time in the canteen. As I made discreet enquiries, they all purported to have been allocated duties which were soon completed… or they simply skived off!

The following morning we were scheduled for a map-reading lecture… yawn… yawn! We decided to melt into the crowd in the canteen but either luck was not with us or we lacked the panache of the habitual lead-swingers and our furtive expressions gave us away. In any event, Lt Cheney, our Company Adjutant was strolling through the canteen and spotted me…

"What are you doing here, Flint? You should be at the lecture on 'B' Deck!"

"Lecture, sir?" I blustered feebly. "I… er… I was…" Desperately I searched for a cover-story which would be convincing yet impossible to check out. There must have been many such for the canteen was heaving with idlers.

"You're skiving, Flint!" he yelled. "You're on a charge… Company Orders tomorrow morning. Now get off to 'B' Deck!"

The pompous, jumped-up little bastard strode off, duty done while I, fuming and mortified, made my way to 'B' Deck.

I mumbled explanations and excuses to a fresh-faced Second-Looey who was standing before an Ordinance Survey map pinned to a blackboard. On the deck, at his feet, a group of bored squaddies sat or sprawled awaiting enlightenment. I took the only revenge which seemed possible...

"Now, can any of you chaps tell me... what is a map?"

My hand shot up like a shuttle launch. "A map is a representation of a piece of countryside drawn to scale...Sah!" I snapped.

"Good lord!" he sputtered, looking at his 'life-line', the army's *Ladybird Book of Elementary Map-Reading for Public-School Pillocks*'. "You know, that's exactly what it says here! Well done, private, jolly good."

From then on, he never had a prayer. I shot his embarrassed, ill-prepared lecture to pieces. I was the archetypal class swot... I answered every question; I blurted out answers when he tried to choose someone else. I quoted the manual at every turn and virtually commandeered his lecture thus making him look inadequate. I forgot to mention that, having studied map-reading at school, I had given a couple of lectures myself!

My childish 'vengeance' did not, however, prevent my being marched before the Company Commander the next morning...

"Left...right...left...right...halt! Cap off! Stand at ease!"

The charge was read out and the sentence passed... seven days 'confined to ship'!

Peter Flint

Disbelief and my ever-present sense of the ridiculous struggled with my anxiety. 'Confined to ship'? We were several hundred miles from land in the middle of the Indian Ocean! What did he expect me to do... stroll over to the nearest pub or cinema? I'm sure you've heard the old joke... "I don't care who your dad is... don't walk across this lake again while I'm fishing!"

Now we come to the reason that this pathetic attempt to dodge a dreary basic map-reading lecture has haunted me the rest of my life. When scoffing at such a ridiculous punishment, I had forgotten a very significant fact... during my enforced week aboard we were to dock at Singapore and Hong-Kong! And so, your foolish, conceited cartographer, (whom, you will remember, had never been anywhere more exciting than Blackpool), would not be going ashore!

I stood watching the lights of Singapore and a few days later, Hong Kong from the deck of the boat, realising that I was missing a once in a lifetime experience. I also knew that the commanding officer was not going to come across to me and say, "We know you're really a good boy so we've decided to let you off... just this once!"

Jankers in the army works on the simple principle... 'O.K. so you wanted to mess the army around... now we'll show you who can really mess people around!' For the periods you are on jankers your life is not your own... your life is not your own anyway in the army but on jankers it is even less your own! From the time you wake up until after the time you go to bed you are harried and hustled.

"Parade outside the Orderly Room at seven-thirty a.m. for inspection!" ... five minutes later... "Parade in denims for work in the kitchens!"

A few years ago we were introduced to the concept of 'meat mountains' and 'butter mountains' but have you ever seen one of the peaks of produce? Neither have I but I have seen a 'pea mountain'! Twelve hundred men get through a hell of a lot of peas at one meal and I found myself shelling peas by the hundred-weight...... there is a military joke there... you know, *shelling* peas... but after five or six hours of monotonous, back-breaking work, the idea loses all essence of humour.

Things got better... I was detailed to sweep the deck. Do you realise that keep-fit fanatics on world cruises can easily jog miles round a ship's deck? Still, it was in the fresh air and peaceful... almost all my mates were losing their money or their 'cherries' in the garish night-spots of Hong Kong... lucky sods!

Things got worse... There are technically no kitchens on a ship... there is a galley. If you do not know what a galley slave is, I am about to tell you... The men who find their way into the Army Catering Corps frequently resemble the food they provide. They are often fat, greasy, unimaginative and whilst their workplaces are usually clean, their persons are not always so.

If you can imagine a goblin... a homunculus created from grease and encrusted grime, you will be approaching the mental picture of the creature whose assistant I was condemned to be for one day of my incarceration. He was the ship's 'plongeur' whose job was to wash the trays, pans, and utensils from which the cholesterol-rich cuisine had been served.

His lair was a metal box scarcely larger than a good-sized wardrobe, alongside the main galley. Had the ship sunk and lain in Davey Jones' Locker for centuries subject to the corrosive effects of millions of gallons of sea-water, this cubicle would have survived unscathed coated as it was with a thick coat of compacted, black grease.

Along one wall of this dark cell were two galvanised troughs filled with a glutinous, lukewarm soup upon which floated all manner of: bits of food; pieces of fat; half-eaten potatoes; cabbage leaves; cigarette butts and other detritus too evil to detail. Along the other three walls lay piles of large, blackened containers of all shapes and sizes which were to be washed in the tepid sludge I have described.

Hours I toiled and sweated, harried and bullied by this grizzled, greasy goblin who, having been formerly the lowest of the low, now found himself in a position of power over an inferior being... me! Endlessly, I plunged grease-coated, charred containers into the two tanks, scrubbing and scraping at them with a sort of wooden lavatory brush. This seemed to have been designed more to paint them all with a further layer of slimy coagulation than remove it. All the time a procession of cooks, scullions and hobble-dee-hoys hurled clattering, clanging used pans onto the shelves as fast as I attempted to clean them... faster!

* * *

Hamlet begins with a line... 'For this relief much thanks!' when he volunteers to do guard-duty on the battlements of Elsinor Castle. I'd always thought... 'What a pillock!'... volunteering to wander about, tired and alone, in the dreary watches of the night but I soon discovered that guard-duty had its compensations.

To you uninitiated civilians, the idea of guarding an enormous ship in the middle of the China Sea might just seem a tad ludicrous. After all, who is likely to pinch... a ship? O.K. so we now have the Somali pirates but you catch my drift... I mean the vessel of which I write accommodated fifteen hundred plus armed, trained warriors... and yours truly! The opportunist thief can hardly take a quick, furtive look over his shoulder; hot-wire it and screech away to some seedy, back-street garage where it can be re-sprayed and emerge as a forty-thousand ton family saloon... only four million miles on the clock... one careful, lady driver... However, the army take no chances!

Two hours on and four hours off... that is the pattern of guard-duty in the army. Two hours of mind-clogging boredom patrolling seeking a potential enemy whom you are well aware exists only in the tortured psyches of the officer class. At times, even the relief of movement is denied and the guard stands motionless in a carefully-selected spot where no enemy can possibly miss seeing him. As an additional assistance for the short-sighted foe, he is required to burnish every conceivable part of his person, his attire and equipment, so that he gleams like a beacon.

In spite of these disadvantages, there was, for me a compensating factor... four out of every six hours when I could sleep, read, write letters, chat to my mates, drink tea and eat buns in the N.A.A.F.I. canteen. Moreover... and here is the crux... I could not be called upon to: shell peas, sweep the decks, 'wash' pans or rush around at the beck and call of every egotistical arse with stripes on his arm or pips on his shoulder.

With this in mind, I volunteered to do the guard-duty of any of my comrades who had the misfortune to draw the short straw. In the course of my seven days' jankers, I did four guard-duties which in comparison to the possible alternatives were almost relaxation.

At two o'clock in the morning on one of my 'stags', as the two-hour periods of duty were called, I witnessed a bizarre event and gained a bonus... I saw time disappear, vanish, evaporate on the instant before my eyes. In 1755, eleven days were removed from the calendar in order to compensate for a long-standing mathematical error... the shibboleth had it that this caused a panic among people who believed that their lives had been shortened by eleven days. Perhaps I, too, should sue the M.O.D. as the army shortened my life by one hour for suddenly the hands of the clock spun forward an hour to indicate three o'clock.

For a moment I was flabbergasted; then I realised what must have happened... the ship had crossed the line denoting a time-zone and the captain had adjusted all the ship's clocks accordingly. I was able, with a clear conscience, to return to the guardroom; waken the luckless squaddie who had the next 'stag' and climb gratefully into my bunk. I never did get that hour back but such is the time elapsed, that I doubt if a combination of Army Intelligence and M.I.5 could trace it!

A less pleasant memory of my week's guard now surfaces. The bunks upon which we slept... when not driven by the heat and the stench to sleep on the deck under the stars... were made of tubular metal and in tiers of three. My normal bunk was in the middle tier and I merely had to swing my legs out and drop a foot or so to the deck. On one of my guard-duties, I was sound asleep on the top bunk in the guardroom when the corporal of the guard shook me saying, "Come on, Flinty... move yourself... you're on stag!"

Half-asleep, I mumbled, "Yes corp..." I swung my legs over the side and dropped. Instead of the foot drop to the deck, it was at least four feet and the added momentum brought my head forward into painful, bloody contact with one of the ship's metal beams.

"Christ! Are you alright, Flinty?" asked the corporal, surveying my blood-streaked face.

I remember murmuring, "England expects corp... I'm going out now... I may be some time!"

* * *

I well recall the crashing surf on the dazzling beach at Colombo in Ceylon... sorry, Shri Lanka. I also remember the bustle, confusion and energy of Hong Kong harbour; the breathtaking ride on the funicular with the city dropping away and the opulent white house and the green hills rushing to meet us. I can still picture my young self gazing over the wooded hills of the New Territories and thinking that beyond lay the vastness of China and its then hostile millions.

Japan is beautiful. The white prow of the ship pushed forward through the dark blue of the sea and was in the middle of a breathtaking scatter of green jewels... the islands of Japan. It is small wonder that Japanese culture prizes serenity, for as we progressed, islands rose before us tranquil and beautiful. It was difficult for me, even then, to associate this peaceful land with the murderous, fanatical race of my juvenile nightmares.

Japan fascinated me... the dress, the language, the buildings, the ancient culture, the chubby, dark-eyed babies gazing curiously at me from their perch on their mothers' backs. Despite the horrors we as peoples had inflicted on each other, curiously, I felt safer and more at home than in any of our erstwhile colonies.

Our battalion was to replace the Durham Light Infantry on Korea's front line. According to rumour, the troops were no longer living in the trenches but in permanent wooden-floored tents. Why am I trying to describe these for you? I'm sure most of you will have seen 'MASH' and become familiar with Hawkeye and Beejay's hidey-hole. Korea, we knew, was colder than Medusa's mammaries and the prospect of facing sub-zero temperatures in a grown-up version of a Boy Scouts' camp appealed to me not at all. Most of the lads in my battalion had no choice but, like good old Uncle Sam, good old Elizabeth Regina decreed that no nasty foreigners were allowed to disembowel you or blast you into bleeding shreds until you had celebrated your nineteenth birthday... such consideration... such humanity!

I found myself, to my delight, with the under-nineteens who were to be fattened up... er... toughened up for the slaughter... er... I mean, the heroic struggle against the evils of communist totalitarian world domination. We callow youths were to hone our combat training at the Miya Jima Battle School. I was acutely aware that, despite the peace talks, the war was merely smouldering and could burst out again at any moment.

We had settled into our temporary quarters... barrack blocks built for the Australian troops stationed in

Peter Flint

Japan after World War II. Within a few days we were to march the twenty or so miles to the battle-school where we would learn to run and crawl across terrain raked by real machine-gun fire without turning a hair… the condition of our under-garments was never discussed! We… the ones amongst us who could count to twelve… with our boots on that is, were not looking forward to the experience. When the Company Sergeant Major asked if anyone had worked in an office, I sprang to attention smartish.

"Two years in the Civil Service…Sah!" I bellowed.

"Can you type, laddie?"

My mind raced… my knowledge of typing was confined to typing my name… once… on one of the machines in the office back home. However, I noticed a smart-looking lance-jack further along the ranks who was also putting himself forward for MY job.

"Type, sir? Of course I can type, sir…"

To this day I'm grateful he didn't ask about Pitman or QUERTY or there would have been a distinct possibility that, when he discovered that I was lying, I would not have had any 'goolies' for the bitter Korean winter to freeze off!

I learned to type rapidly… I'll rephrase that… I rapidly learned to type slowly and settled down to a fascinating year in Japan.

It was not all sake and geishas but at least it was warm, dry and, unlike my less-fortunate comrades, I did not have to pray that whoever lined up those machine-guns to fire just above the heads of the rookies at the battle-school, was at least able to keep his socks on while counting a dozen eggs. If... no... *when*... I finally get round to typing this epic, I shall still rely on the Peteman four-two typing method... four fingers and two thumbs!

* * *

Many years after I left the army, I was invited by a friend, who was an R.A.F. officer, to attend his station's Summer Ball. It was an elaborate occasion... no expense spared... full evening dress, at which I arrived very hung over and left at four thirty in the morning stone cold sober but that's another story. As it was derigeur to wear the 'full fig' could I wear my medal...

"Medal? You've got a medal?" he enquired, half-dubious and half-envious.

"Of course," I replied, "hasn't everyone?"

I still recall with sneaky glee the envious, questioning glances of the young R.A.F. pilots as I sauntered around the mess, my 'Butcher's Apron' sneering at their, as yet, undecorated bosoms. 'What' you are asking... at least, I *hope* you are asking, 'What feat of derring-do did I perform to be awarded a medal?'

Actually, I got it as a post-script to a bollocking... if that's not too unfortunate a choice of words... about the number of lads who had 'copped for a dose'… er… caught V.D. No, I did not get a medal for NOT catching V.D… it happened this way……

Back home in the U.K. in that era, for most of us, sex was holding hands with your girlfriend in the back row of the cinema. It was 'safe sex' too as short white gloves were very chique at that time! In Japan we soon discovered that sex was readily available and it was for sale! There were snags… three snags to be precise. Most of us didn't really know where it was… what to do when we found it or whether; having negotiated numbers one and two; we were prepared for our treasured members to rot off slowly at the root.

There were those among us who through experience, lust or recklessness gave no thought to the morrow and sought the many bars, brothels and back-streets where, for a few yen, one could 'lose one's cherry'. The army had no illusions about soldiers' sexual habits or about the reduction in military efficiency caused by soldiery with suppurating weapons. The army, therefore, provided, next to the guard-room, a little room, euphemistically called, the 'Prophylactics Clinic' where there were… free of charge condoms to collect before and various creams and unguents to decontaminate the willy afterwards.

To their cost, it appeared that a number of privates had not been protecting their privates resulting in an epidemic of 'spotted-dick'. Hence, the bollocking… sorry… that word again!

Our Company Commander, having described at length the munificence of Her Majesty's forces in providing contraception... the searing torment the culprits would endure... even if they did not contract V.D., said, "Oh... and by the way... you shower of shit have been here two weeks... go down to the Quarter-Master's Stores and draw your medals..." Ah well... 'Dulce et dickorum est...!'

* * *

I did not get on with my sergeant...perhaps getting on with a sergeant is a contradiction in terms. Sergeant Parry was a child of the army... literally and metaphorically. He had enlisted as a boy-soldier at an unbelievably early age and the army had been family, home and mother to him from then on. The more perceptive of you will have noticed that I omitted to mention his father!

He... Sergeant Parry... that is was dark, lean and immaculate. He had clawed his way up from the ranks by native wit and determination. I always felt that he resented my grammar school education and rather unmilitary attitudes. At all events, he gave me a hard time... bullying, sarcastic and threatening in a manner which he never seemed to employ with the other two lads who worked in the Documents Office under his command. He was constantly threatening to have me posted back to the battalion in Korea... a potent threat for the reasons I have already chronicled. In fact, I never did achieve the

Peter Flint

security of being a permanent member of the staff at J.R.B.D. as the camp was called.

However, despite Parry's snarls and jibes and the Damoclean fate of frostbite in the battalions, the sprung mattress, good food, camp cinema, sports-field and 'swimming-pool', made it worthwhile.

Unfortunately, disasters are not uncommon in Japan... earthquakes, typhoons and volcanoes are among the natural hazards of this otherwise beautiful country. It was because of this that I was sent to the battle-school to learn to operate a C90 Radio as a Disaster Net was being established among all the allied bases...

We sat... some twenty of us... in a classroom resembling a school physics laboratory. In front of each of us sat the radio; an olive green metal box at least three feet long. Nowadays, the footsloggers of the P.B.I. have satellite communication, infra-red night goggles and, for all I know, C.B. Beebees and U-Tube built into their helmets... if not their actual skulls! The Disaster Net portable radio... if you had a jeep... was a monster which bristled with huge bakelite knobs, switches and dials... it looked like something out of the nineteen-thirties space serial 'Flash Gordon'. I suspect that today the case of one of these radios could house the whole of the Japanese electronics industry.

Our guide to the mysteries of ethereal communication was a swarthy French-Canadian sergeant in an olive-green, lightweight uniform emblazoned with colourful heraldic badges and flashes at every visible point. In heavily accented English, he showed us how to modulate the ear-splitting screech to obtain the frequency of the Disaster Net. He explained all the procedures and jargon now so familiar to all T.V. audiences. Then we were allowed to practise sending messages to each other! It was unreal... using all the formula... "Able, Charlie, Foxtrot this Baker, Delta, Oboe" ... "Come in Able, Charlie, Foxtrot..." etc. etc. we would be talking to the guy three feet away on the bench in front!

It was not long before our childish sense of humour and sexually explicit vocabularies produced some highly-volatile messages back and forth across the 'physics lab'. We were thoroughly enjoying our new toys... vying with each other in obscenity and anatomical invention when a stream of New World Gallic invective seared our eardrums...

"You stupeed sheet-heads... you bollock-brained eediots! What zee furk do you sink you are doing? Hein?"

Like the air from an abandoned party-balloon the hilarity hissed out of us to leave us apprehensive and bewildered at the fury of this diminutive demon.

"Do you furking deemweets not realise that all these furking crap wheech you sink is so funnee is being picked urp all overrr these furking contree?"

We realised! It had never occurred to us that an imaginative description of Able, Charlie, Foxtrot's sexual

Peter Flint

endowments was not merely leaping the ether between the two benches but beaming like the B.B.C. News' countdown sequence, to listeners far and wide!

This reminded me of a tale told to me by a former colleague who had served in the regular army during World War II of a similar incident. He had been sending a message by radio and the signal kept coming back, 'Message not understood...' Finally, he got on the phone and asked to speak to the W.A.A.F. radio operator on the other end. When she came on the phone he asked her to go outside and check the radio-aerial. When she asked the reason, he said, "Well, the message is alright when it comes out this end... perhaps your aerial has a bloody knot in it!"

Sometime after the French-Canadian radio farce, I found myself in a beer-hall having a highly intellectual discussion with the sergeant... in French! Considering that, at that time, my French consisted of the dubious daily doings of a super-stereotypical French family and their dreary 'fils' Gaston, this was in itself remarkable.

Following the Disaster Net training, with a... "G'day,sport!" or some other Antipodean farewell, the two Aussies dropped us in a hole! With us they left a radio, two enormous lead-acid batteries and Australian rations for the day. The food at J.R.B.D. was good but this was ambrosia... no... not cream-rice... chicken with tinned peaches to follow!

All day we sat snug in our hole at the top of a pine-studded hill and read old copies of Readers' Digest'. From time to time, we tried to contact other trainee Disaster Netters... to no avail. Fortunately, the day was fine and sunny; the grub was excellent and, to my then unsophisticated literary tastes, the R.D. stories acceptable. I even remember one of the R.D.'s 'jokes'......

Some lads were out camping and started telling horror stories about the size of the mosquitoes they had seen on some of their previous outdoor adventures. The exaggerations got wilder until the quiet one in the group said, "I was camping in Scotland and saw two gigantic mossies hovering over my bed. One said to the other, "Shall we eat him here or should we take him outside?"

As we enjoyed such rib-tickling hilarity, the gods of Fire, Earthquake and Flood slept in the pleasant sunshine. Our enforced radio silence occasioned three visits from the Aussies with new, freshly-charged batteries for the radio but no harbinger of imminent doom oscillated along the airways from our comfy pit. It never occurred to us... nor presumably the instructors at the battle-school... that it might just have been the radio rather than the batteries but in the army, doing absolutely nothing is a rare event so we did not push our good fortune.

From our dugout we did witness a bizarre sight. Skirmishing through the pine trees on the hill to our left were the grey uniforms of the Japanese army while, immediately in front of us, the bleached-khaki of Australian troops also practising the art of war.

Despite the failure of our final radio training exercise, we returned to our office desks in J.R.B.D. as fully-fledged radio operators. Fortunately for us; save for one tremor which shook the barrack-block, caused the lights to swing and, tragically buried two children in a land-slip which hit the village just up the road from the camp; no disasters came our way… at least no natural ones!

* * *

About six of us had drawn a cricket bat, pads and a ball from the camp sports' store and we used them to wile away the hot lunch-hour with an impromptu cricket match between the two barrack-blocks. Imitating Dennis Compton… or some other contemporary sporting hero… Ginger stepped down the pitch and made a perfect off-drive. The ball soared away to crash through the glass of the Regimental Police barrack-room opposite. To add insult to injury, they had the sash-window open because of the heat so it demolished both panes. They were not amused! The next day an edict appeared on Company Orders… 'On no account will cricket be played between the barrack-blocks' signed Major Rhodes, Company Commander.'

Ever, obedient, we six erstwhile, potential Test cricketers trooped down to the sports' store; handed in our bat… our pads… our ball… Then we drew out baseball gloves, bat and ball… well, the order did say specifically, 'No Cricket' didn't it?

You may be wondering what work I did to earn the magnificent two pounds fifty per week that Elizabeth Regina paid me... other than sitting on hillsides in the sun eating tinned peaches and reading iffy jokes from Readers' Digest. Well, Japan was a sort of staging-post for British troops shipping to Korea or returning to postings in Hong Kong, Malaya, and the Middle East or... lucky sods... back home to good old Blighty. A joke current at the time tells of a lad working in the army mail sorting office. He was put on a charge for using foul language... those, dear reader were gentler times. His defence was that he was sorting the mail and saying, "One fo' Korea... another fo' Korea......"

Think about it!

When a troopship arrived in Kure harbour, Sergeant Parry, accompanied by one of we lackeys, went in a jeep and collected all the necessary documents pertaining to the thousand or so souls in transit. Several huge mail-sacks of these documents were dumped onto the floor of our office and we then worked like fury sorting them; bundling them and sending them on to the correct units which were to be the soldiers' next postings.

There were three important documents which accompanied on his travels to the trouble spots of the globe... a list of the kit which had been issued to him... his conduct sheet and his medical record. Invariably we found that over-zealous commanding officers had invented their own forms and, equally invariably, they were screwed into balls and dropped on the floor of the office to be cleared up later. Our office only possessed three files… General… Miscellaneous and the 'B' File…

'B' stood for 'Bin'. When a boat came in from the U.K. the 'B' File was totally inadequate… the office floor would be a foot deep in screwed-up balls of paper saying, "Private Richard Head 2267439 is a crack-shot with a Mark lll Peashooter at eight-hundred yards" …or similar. Hours of testing and meticulous recording ended up as a snowdrift of superfluous bumph filling the whole of the office floor space.

The phone rang…

"Docs Office… Private Flint speaking…"

"Oh, Medical Officer here… just got this detachment of forty chaps from the East Lancs Regiment over here and I can't seem to find their vaccination certificates. I don't suppose you've still got them over there?"

"Don't think so, sir but we'll check our files. I'll give you a ring more scoshi, sir if I find them."

Putting down the phone, I explained the M.O.'s query to the other two lads.

"No, I've not come across them," said Les, slitting open another large buff envelope.

"Nor me," said Ginger, abstracting the three vital documents and screwing up the elaborate certificate embossed with the regimental badge of some highland regiment.

For half an hour or so we worked on, when suddenly amid the mounting heap of debris; a pale, crumpled, buff form caught my eye. Idly I picked it up and smoothed it out...

> "This is to certify that Private Parts has been vaccinated against: small-pox, cholera, yellow-fever...et al."
>
>   Signed: Capt. I. Perdermic,
>
>   Medical Officer...41st Foot and Mouth Regt.

"Shit! Look at this... it's one of those vaccination certificates the M.O. was ringing about."

One by one we found the other thirty-nine, smoothing them as best we could and piling them under a heavy book to remove at least some of the creases.

I picked up the phone... "Captain Rogers? Flint here, sir, Docs Office... we've found those vaccination forms you were trying to track down, sir... the one's you phoned us about. Someone had filed them in a separate envelope, sir... I'll bring them right across immediately, sir."

"Don't bother, old chap. Not to worry... I've vaccinated 'em all again... just to be on the safe side."

Peter Flint

These particular vaccines usually caused at least two days sweating, aching joints and muscles often with swellings in the armpits and nausea. I looked at the almost-smooth pile of buff-coloured forms before filing them under 'B'.

I'm sure that all those nauseous, sweating, swelling, suffering squaddies would have been grateful had they known that we had unwittingly to thank for their being doubly protected from small-pox, cholera, yellow-fever...

* * *

Compared to the typical accommodation we had experienced in the U.K. and certainly what we would have had to put up with in Korea, our quarters in Kure were luxurious. Two-storey white barrack-blocks with two long barrack-rooms on the ground floor, each housing twenty men. There were two identical barrack-rooms on the floor above. They had been built to accommodate Australian troops at the end of World War II when the Japanese had surrendered following the world's first... and only... use of atomic bombs on Hiroshima and Nagasaki some eight years previously. These barrack-rooms were, by our standards, luxurious with sprung beds and thick, sprung mattresses. As I have said, the food was good and plentiful and we had free sports facilities, a cinema and even a large concrete tank which made a perfectly acceptable swimming-pool. We also had rats! It took many sleepless nights and an enormous effort of rationalisation to reconcile normal day-to-day life with the nightly scratching and scuffling in the wall immediately behind your head. Today, I'm sure the tabloids would have had a field-day... "Heroes Sleep with Japanese Rodents!" ... "Our Brave Boys Ratted-On by my M.O.D." ... "Warfare Without Warfarin" etc. There would almost certainly have been irate parents on television and litigation. In those far off days you only had the classic response to complaints by the sergeant in the popular comedy series 'It Ain't Half Hot, Mum!' ... "Oh dear... how sad... never mind!" I can't speak for the other lads but I was never totally reconciled to our Oriental pets but somehow, I came to terms with the situation.

One evening we were all sitting on our beds, chatting, reading, bulling up kit when from behind one of the lockers came a rat! He must have been a trained kamikaze rodent for his dash across the room was made under a hail of boots, brushes, helmets, mess-tins and bayonets!

One night I woke in the wee small hours and to my horror, crawling along the half-inch wide batten directly above my bed was a huge rat! I yelled and sat up like lightning... he ran down my trousers' leg... fortunately, I was not wearing them... they were hanging from a hook at the side of the bed... and he was gone!

My mate, Brian, who slept in the bed next to me, was not so lucky. One night he woke me with a terrified yell and I saw a dark form scurry across his bed and disappear. It turned out that another rat, making the perilous, nocturnal journey along this narrow board, had slipped and fallen onto Brian's face as he lay asleep!

    Nightie...night... sleep well!

Grandad's Army

Report Document #005

LAND OF THE RISING SON...ER...SUN

I suppose we all look back and think, 'If only...'. Japan was, for me, a glorious experience which, by and large, I wasted. Beautiful, intriguing, mysterious and fascinating. I should have learned its language and studied its customs. As it was, I chose to spend free time with my mates in the N.A.A.F.I. or on the sports field.

Unlike many of the lads, I did regularly walk the path through the paddy-fields, over the wooded hills to the little fishing villages with their sun-bleached boats and tiny winding streets. I usually met one or two Japanese women clomping up the steep path on their wooden platform shoes; a sagging bamboo cane across their shoulders with a heavy wooden bucket at either end. Figures like this could be bought in every souvenir shop as a quaint reminder of oriental peasant life. What the souvenir-hunters fail to recognise was the hills were extremely steep; the paths were very rough; the buckets were incredibly heavy and... they were filled to the brim with... human excrement!

This was used to fertilise the high terraces, some only a foot or so wide... they grew some lovely tomatoes! What do

Peter Flint

you put on your tomatoes, granddad? That's funny... we put salad-dressing on ours!

I did make several memorable excursions while I was in Japan so I suppose that my time was not entirely wasted. I spent a week's leave in Tokyo: a bustling, garish, neon city even then. We did several touristy things... the Imperial Palace, the Ginza Market, a huge temple that was beautifully painted in black and orange, housing thousands of wooden spoons! These ranged from the ordinary domestic pudding-stirrers to giants some ten or twelve feet long. Trouble-makers in the army were known as 'shit-stirrers'... Until I saw this temple, I never realised that they had their own religion!

We also visited a delightful park with tinkling streams; maple-shadowed paths overlooking serene pools crossed by arched, wooden bridges. I remember the tranquillity of the Buddhist monastery with its immaculately-raked, gravel beds and elegant rocks placed like peaceful islets in a geometric ocean. There, too, I marvelled at the fragile perfection of a two-hundred-year-old bonsai tree.

The bustle of the Tokyo streets in contrast to my small home town and the tiny fishing villages I have described absolutely fascinated me. Not yet was it the centre of the global electronics industry nor did its tiny policemen, like miniaturised American T.V. cops, have to breath bottled oxygen periodically when on traffic duty because of the pollution. Still, looking back, the signs were already there.

However, even in that far-off land, the immutable laws of human mischance pertain. We were trying to find one of Tokyo's landmarks and, as our command of the language was slim... very slim... we were pleased to see, coming towards us, a G.I. with his Japanese girlfriend.

"Say, Mac," we asked... we knew from our film-going that all Americans were called Mac... "Could the lady tell us how we get to the Ernie Pyle Theatre?"

He turned to his girlfriend who replied in perfect Bronx English, "Gee honee... I don't have the slightest idea... sorreeee!"

In general, the Japanese are small people but, walking along a crowded street in Tokyo, I saw giants! The street was jostling with sightseers, shoppers, workers, when, like two enormous liners nosing their way through a fleet of coracles, came two Sumo wrestlers. Each towered over the folk around him; they were huge men with the traditional Samurai pigtail. They wore black kimonos, tied at the waist with the distinctive sashes of their craft.

The Tokyo Police Judo Academy was a revelation... Being one of the nerdy 'before' specimens who was always getting the sand kicked in his face in the old Charles Atlas body-building ads, I secretly desired the knowledge and the skill which would enable me, with a flick of the wrist to send bullies and other evil-doers flying through windows or smashing into furniture. At one of the world's most prestigious judo schools, I expected to be dodging flying bodies... some frozen in mid-air... much as one ducks and weaves to avoid a persistent wasp.

The hall was huge... light and airy with a floor of the plaited, straw matting found in Japanese homes. Scattered across its pale surface were seemingly hundreds of pairs of white-clad, grunting, jerking, heaving figures. Nowhere did I see the elegant wrist-flick, sending the opponent into humiliating orbit. Occasionally, a pair of straining grunters would lash around violently for a second or two and one would crash to the floor having been felled by the sweeping leg-slice known to footballers as the professional foul. I suppose there was a lesson there for me that when faced with baddies who are bigger than you, if you have not put in all the grunting, heaving, hard work and dedication, the only sensible course is to run!

To lure western visitors to Japan, the tourist posters often show the Torri at Miyajima. The photograph is usually taken at sunset with the soft, green hills darkening into shadow and the burning red disk sinking into a sea of molten bronze. Silhouetted against this dramatic backdrop, the exquisite drooping arch of the 'god gate' stands in the sea.

My last week in Japan was spent in this magical spot. I had been given a travel warrant and a ten-day leave pass to the R & R camp at Miyajima. I set off with just fifteen pence in my pocket, so sudden had been this piece of luck.

The corner seat of my railway carriage was by a crumpled, dishevelled Aussie with whom I fell into the following conversation...

"Where you off to then, mate?" he asked.

"Ten days leave... C.O. only told me yesterday... still, better than working eh?"

"Yeah," he replied, "too right."

"You on leave?"

"Just been... Tokyo... ten days. Just going back to my unit then back home to Oz."

"You lucky bugger! Had a good time?"

"Had a great time... blew a hundred and ten quid in ten days," he said, a dreamy smile on his face.

I thought of MY week's spending money... fifteen pence!

"Jesus!" I gasped. "A hundred and ten quid! Still, if you're going home, you'll have bought presents for your family and that..."

"Presents? Oh yeah... I got 'em some real beaut presents."

"How much did they set you back?"

His brow furrowed, calculating. "Between ten and twenty quid... I reckon."

"Bloody hell... ten and twenty quid! What did you spend the rest on mucker?"

"Beer and women..." he sighed with the smile of a satisfied customer.

This story becomes more incredible when you think that the average weekly wage for a private soldier in the British Army at that time was about two pounds!

Miyajima is a holy island. It had one rambling, wooden fishing village where no one is born and no one dies! Before you rush out to buy a plane ticket and set off in search of immortality, I should explain... As Miyajima is a holy island, ladies who are about to give birth, are transferred the short distance to the mainland as are people who are terminally ill. Doubtless there have been 'accidents' at both ends of the lifecycle but it still is a lovely idea.

There were several shrines on the island... oh... and a white horse. No he wasn't the one who went into a pub and ordered a pint whereupon the astonished landlord said, "We've got a brand of whisky name after you."

"What... Eric?" said the horse.

Legend has it that all animals given to the gods on Miyajima turn white. I don't know what colour Eric-san was when he first made the crossing but he was certainly the designated white colour when I saw him. Also he had a real cushy number as hundreds of Japanese tourists paraded past his pen to pat his nose and give him sweets, apples and little dishes of oats which could be purchased at a kiosk nearby. There was also a large paddock with a herd of 'sacred' deer. The magic had worked for Eric-san but the deer had remained stubbornly deer-coloured.

One night my pal and I were returning after a debauch in the village… you can imagine the extent of the debauchery one could buy for fifteen pence… even in the Japan of nineteen fifty-four… the comparison with my Aussie 'mate' is astonishing.

It was late… dark and alien. Once we had left the dim lights of the village, we had a mile or so of dirt road to cover before the brighter lights of the camp appeared. Somewhat apprehensively we skirted Eric-san's stall and crossed the silent square in front of the shadowy, lowering Buddhist temple. Suddenly there was a rustle… then a rattle… then a clatter in the darkness. Our hearts leapt and we swung our eyes nervously towards the mysterious temple. Gazing at us from a candle-lit alcove was an impassive figure!

All the terrifying nightmares of the unknown sped through my mind in the instant before I realised that our silent observer was merely a statue of Buddha, dressed in silken robes and set in a niche illuminated by flickering night-lights. The noise which had sent our pulse-rate into overdrive had been the deer, aroused from a well-earned sleep, milling around in their pen.

Peter Flint

Possibly the most beautiful building on Miyajima was the floating shrine. A long, low, wooden building, beautifully painted and graced with the traditional concave arches of Japanese tradition, it does seem to float like a jewel in the setting of dark pines and placid sea. In fact, it is built on piles sunk into the seabed but, like the Torri, this illusory separation from the solidity of earth imparts an unworldliness lacking in more mundane settings.

I was told that it was to this shrine that the young Japanese pilots who had dedicated their lives to their god and emperor as part of 'The Holy Wind… Kamikaze'… came to receive their last rites. After a period of veneration and indulgence they went to the shrine at Miyajima for a ceremony of purification before their final flight to oblivion. I have read that in the initial stages, volunteers came joyfully and in numbers but that as the euphoria following the attack on Pearl Harbour evaporated, the under-carriage on the planes fell away immediately after take off thus eliminating any change of mind by preventing a normal landing.

Passing this shrine one evening, I was attracted by the curious plink-plonk note of a stringed instrument in counterpoint to the gentle plash of the waves lapping against the piles. I crept closer to see a small audience sitting, Japanese fashion, in a tiny amphitheatre in the courtyard of the shrine. To the eerie music of the stringed instrument, white faces blank and impassive, the actors, clad in gorgeous, richly-embroidered costumes and head-dresses, moved through their stylised, robotic ritual like life-sized porcelain dolls. I stood gazing fascinated yet afraid, not sure whether I was witnessing a traditional folk-play or intruding on a mysterious and sacred ceremony.

* * *

Remember the rats? Well this next ale is also concerned with creepy-crawlies so the squeamish among you should read this next bit with your eyes closed. At the leave camp we were quartered in tents… these were not the leaky, clumsy, masochistic canvas punishment sacks favoured by tough outdoor folk and boy scouts… these had wooden floors, electric lights and comfortable beds complete with mosquito-nets. Mosquito-nets, as the name suggests, are eminently practical and essential in certain foreign lands but have acquired a romantic image of raffish, white-suited ex-pats in seedy, steamy hotels bubbling with intrigue and dark dealings or heroic expeditions to find the mysterious lost city at the source of the Donwanago River or subdue the beastly pagans on the Khyber Pass.

Feeling like Humphrey Bogart or Errol Flynn, I stretched out luxuriously in my 'cot'… they're never 'beds' in these Boys' Own Adventure tales. A pale light filtered through the taut canvas of the tent and the folds of my protective canopy. On the netting just above my head was a large, dark blob which I took to be a tangle of ends where the strips of netting had been sewn. Idly, I poked the blob with my finger… and it moved! Would you believe it? So did I… fast!

Trying not to dislodge the moving whatever it was, I slid like a limbo-dancer under the net and out of the bed. I switched on the light. Now I could see 'it' solid and black inside the net. Gingerly, I pulled the net to the side and shook it. The 'thing' fell to the floor and waddled off steadily like a portly cleric. What was 'it'? Oh, didn't I say? It was some species of stag-beetle… over three inches long and with a pair of pincers with which it could have cut through a chain-link fence!

* * *

The delicate, china bowl held a clear, cold liquid like weak tea from the centre of which gazed up at me, like an accusing eye, a raw egg-yolk! Probably today I would have tried this Japanese delicacy with interest or enthusiasm but this was in an age when beef-burgers were exotic. My introduction to Japanese cuisine… now 'cool' in sushi bars in most cities in the U.K… was not propitious, nor was the occasion.

Sergeant Parry had withdrawn a considerable sum from his army credits. This was a system whereby the army ensured the solvency of its personnel by withholding a portion of the soldier's pay as savings at the squaddie's own request. Sergeant Parry had, we gathered, accumulated sufficient 'credits' since joining to buy his own army should he have so wished. Some tiny spark of camaraderie and humanity must have flickered in his adamantine heart for he had raided his treasure chest and proposed to take his favourite underlings on a weekend break. Needless to say, I was excluded but, in true musketeer spirit, my two pals said either I went or Parry went alone. I am eternally grateful for this show of solidarity as it initiated one of my most treasured memories… Hiroshima!

The hotel was clean and uncluttered… my experience of hotels at this period was, I'll admit limited… this was the first hotel to welcome me. I had expected a futon on the floor but found a normal bed… immaculately clean and comfortable with a small, chunky, brightly-coloured pillow. I took off my boots and flopped back luxuriously onto the bed and the plump, inviting pillow only to sit up feeling slightly dazed as I discovered that the pillow was packed hard and solid with beans!

My enduring memory of this tragically historic spot is of a large, bustling city, indistinguishable in many ways from those of the west… not a flimsy shanty town of wood and paper as many may imagine.

I recall thinking that human beings will find a way to exploit even the most horrific, inconceivable disaster when I saw a souvenir shop next to the empty shell of the building above which the bomb detonated. This tiny shop, run by a survivor, sold mementos of the evil day when Armageddon fell from a clear, blue sky. I looked at the photographs of the aftermath of the bomb… a toy by today's standards and tried to relate the level wasteland

Peter Flint

of shattered rubble and human desolation with the busy spot on which I stood.

Three images have stayed with me of that little shop in a dusty corner of Hiroshima. A photograph of the proprietor showed his back seared and scarred by the devil's whiplash of blast and flame. Secondly, a piece of stone carried the black, shadowy form of a human being photographed... not burned... photographed by the intensity of the flash before the heat vaporised him or her. Finally, I remember three heavy terra-cotta roof tiles which had been fired in a kiln... these had been melted and twisted together by the immense heat!

I stood in the shell of the peace memorial with its simple, poignant plaque... 'Let there be no more Hiroshimas' and gazed through the empty, metal ribs of the dome at the innocent sky. I tried to imagine the scene as it had been just eight years before... the blinding light... the scorching heat... the horrendous force of the blast. Thousands upon thousands of ordinary human lives snuffed out on the instant. I looked at the busy streets and the quiet flow of the river and tried to picture the badly-burnt survivors leaping into its waters to ease their agony only to find that it was boiling!

Today I heard the television news talk of an agreement between Russia and America to reduce the number of nuclear warheads... each infinitely more powerful than the one which destroyed Hiroshima. I think again of that devastated city and of Nagasaki and Chernobyl and ask what worm of madness lives in the human psyche to allow such evil to exist...

* * *

As I write polish this narrative up for you lovely readers to enjoy, this week, (July 2013) the North Koreans celebrated the sixtieth anniversary of the end of the Korean War... with a parade of goose-stepping troops, tanks and rockets! They, like Iran, have been warned about their attempts to obtain nuclear weapons. I mean, as we all know; only the 'Good Guys' are permitted to have these monstrous, ridiculous devices!

Peter Flint

CHERRY RIPE...

This is the part of the story you've been waiting for... you know... the torrid tales of sizzling sex from the land of the rising son... er... sun. Perhaps you should just flip over these next few pages if you are expecting something sensual, imaginative and revealing. In fact, there is far more excitement in the appendix to this book... 'Japanese Cookery for the Unimaginative' including 'Sukiyake for the Over-Sixties' and 'A Hundred and One Things to do with an Octopus'.

Sex was something we thought about frequently... er... constantly but performed rarely... if at all! The sexual mores of the fifties seemed based on the principle that nice girls didn't and naughty girls did but then your willy dropped off. At least this was the message conveyed to we lusty lads... complete with V.D... 'O' nasties in glorious technicolour.

Thus it was, that a bunch of lads who could get an erection watching Doris Day taking her gloves off or trying to imagine what Jane Russell kept in a bra which looked like two scale models of the Great Pyramid, found ourselves in a country where 'a short time' cost fifteen pence and an 'all-nighter'... including beer and breakfast, cost about a pound!

Some lads lost their 'cherries', as their virginity was called, almost before the crew had time to haul up the gangplank of the troopship upon which they had arrived in Japan. Others... myself included... were like kids in a sweetie shop. We drooled over the goodies but our Mams had told us not to touch!

Our first experience of sex for sale came... alright... *occurred*... in Aden. Three of us wandered down the hot, dusty streets unable to believe our eyes... it was just like all the films we had ever seen. Swarthy men in flowing robes chatted and haggled; shrouded women hurried by. Baskets, piled with wares, lay scattered on the sun-baked street and camels sneered their way through a chaos of traffic.

Suddenly, we were accosted by a small boy... an urchin aged about eight or nine who tugged at my sleeve demanding, "You want woman, Johnny? Me take you... very clean... very cheap. Come Johnny..."

Indeed we did 'want women' but as supermarkets had not yet arrived in Britain, the idea of the 'impulse buy' was alien to us. We were like curates in a sex-shop... shocked and excited simultaneously. Years of conditioning told.

"You dirty little sod!" we cried. "No, we don't want a woman... fuck off before I clout you!"

The little lad probably didn't understand a word... well, perhaps a couple of them! He scurried off to find less inhibited clients for his wares... er... should that read 'whores'?

By the time we got to Colombo a week or so later, the gaucheness of our somewhat puritanical upbringing had begun to fray just a little. We were sharing a large ripe pineapple, yellow and dripping with juice, which we had bought from a street vendor. We had been warned of forbidden fruit... both literally and metaphorically but the pineapple was just too tempting.

A young man stood before us, a dazzling smile on his olive face. "Hello Johnny... you want see exhibition... only ten rupees?"

"What exhibition?"

"Very naughty... very interesting... woman fuckee-fuckee with donkey."

Our jaws dropped and our eyes widened... 'You want woman?' was one thing... this was unbelievable!

"Where is this exhibition then, mate?"

"Little way. You come... me show you. Very naughty... only ten rupees..."

41.

We were nervous... ambush, robbery, murder all vied with our testosterone-fuelled curiosity. Besides, there were four of us... all trained warriors... surely we safe enough?

"O.K. Johnny... you show." Notice how we had not only learned the language but knew the name of all the native male population.

The youth darted away down side streets and alleys until we came to a street lined with crumbling white houses.

"Is here..." he said. "I go arrange exhibition. You give me ten rupee... you wait five minutes... I come back."

I'd like to say... later I did say... that I knew exactly what was going to happen but, truth to tell, I was afraid to enter the dark doorway and the idea of bestiality nauseated me even at that time. There are few occasions when I have not regretted my wimpishness and this was one such.

I watched my three mates enter the building as I sat thinking of all manner of possibilities. About fifteen minutes later, they emerged and walked towards me muttering angrily.

"What's up," I asked. "Er... what was it like... er... you know... the exhibition?"

I expected to be teased and chivvied mercilessly for my faint-heartedness but their anger was not at me.

"We've been shafted... that's what! Took ten fucking bob off of each of us he did. Told us to wait while he got things sorted then the little cunt fucked off didn't he?"

I found it hard not to grin and gloat but asked, "Where did he go?"

"He must have scarpered out the back. Left us standing in this shitty hall like a right load of twats!"

I didn't know for whom I felt most sorry... them or the phantom lady or the mythical donkey!

* * *

There were prostitutes everywhere in Kure. The pretty, over-painted 'hostesses' in all the beer-halls would not only bring your drinks but would take you back to their place for a 'short-time' or all night when the bar closed.

Prostitutes lined the main street in ones and twos or small groups. We quickly learned to evade the tugging hand... rebuff the brazen question or reject the tired appeal.

One evening, a group of us stood chatting on a street corner when one of the prostitutes half-pushed... half-sidled into our midst.

"You want 'short-time'... I shagging very good... very nice?"

Most of us grinned and shook our heads but Jock was far less genteel.

"Och, fuck off!" he said in his strong Glaswegian accent. "You'se fucking ugly!"

The poor woman was not young and certainly no beauty but she was a match for Jock. Pointing at her face, she said, "Face-o number ten!" She paused, then with exquisite timing, she pointed to her vagina and said, "Number One!"

Even then she did not make a sale but she had coined a catch-phrase which haunted the barrack-room for weeks afterwards.

The availability of sex on the streets and in the numerous beer-halls is well-illustrated by an incident which occurred at the battle school where, you may recall, I was being trained to warn people of the arrival of earthquakes, typhoons and tidal waves...as if one wouldn't notice!

As the disaster net incorporated allied units from all over Japan, we were a motley crew... (Why are crews always motley?)... Who lay, smoking and chatting in the half-darkness of the hut. Certainly none was more motley than "Little and Large"... an enormous, military policeman... well over six feet and built like a breeze-block outbuilding and a tiny, wispy, Yorkshire Terrier of a man from some decidedly un-manly outfit... R.A.S.C., Pay Corps or the like.

"Where you stationed then?" asked the giant.

"Maintenance Section... Hiro," answered the terrier.

"We're near there an' all... some fucking great beer-halls down Hiro, eh?"

"Yeah... 'Silver Moon'... 'Nancy's Place'... you get in there?"

"Yeah... they're O.K. The bints in there are pretty good... aren't they?"

"Yeah... not bad. Do you know Alice in 'The Silver Moon'?"

"Aye... reckon I've seen her a time or two," said the M.P.

"Mind you," said the terrier, "the 'Sake House' is the best I reckon."

"Yeah, I get in the 'Sake House' meself regular... some fucking gorgeous crumpet in there..."

"'S funny so do I ... not seen you in there though have I?" He laughed. "Not likely to miss a bloke your size!"

"Wednesdays and Saturdays I usually get down there... got a bird down there."

"You say you've got a regular girl down there then?"

"Yeah... she's great... got a house about three streets away. Breakfast... gets me beer in and that... bath... great... better than being at home. Except for the missus and kids of course."

"O' course," said the terrier in the reverential tones we lads in the mob always used for the squeaky-clean, Debbie

Peter Flint

Reynolds icons back in the Promised Land... Blighty! "Eh, I've got a bint down there as well."

"Well, fuck me sideways... have you?"

"S'pect she'll know yours... what's she like?"

"Short hair...sort of clipped... roundish face..."

"Short cropped hair, you say... does she talk with a sort of a funny accent like?"

"Now you come to mention it, she's does... sort of Yankee twang... used to work over at the Canadian Depot..."

Like a giant volcano, the huge policeman began to rumble with laughter. "Well, fuck me backwards," he kept muttering between chuckles. "What did you say her name was again?"

"It's Lucy... that's not her real Japanese name o' course but everybody calls her Lucy... why?"

By now all the hut lay tuned in to this conversation far more accurately than to any of the net's frequencies.

"Which nights did you say you went with her... Lucy...then?"

"Usually Mondays and Tuesdays... I've got regular shifts... oh fucking Nora..."

By now they had both started to roar with laughter.

"Well fuck me! We're both shagging the same bint on different nights, aren't we?"

Grandad's Army

This is a true story and there is a philosophical message to it... 'Greater love hath no man than he lay down his lay for his neighbour!'

Have you ever hovered before a particularly hair-raising ride at a fairground? You want to experience the thrill and excitement but feel the ice-cube settle in your stomach as you steel yourself to the decision to buy a ticket. Many times in Japan I felt this strange mixture of emotions like the moment when you step past the smiling air-hostess into the belly of the plane and realise that the die is cast!

Sergeant Parry and my two pals were in the Hiroshima hotel playing cards. I have always found card-games, board-games and the like tedious in the extreme so I decided to go out for a walk. I now live in a tiny village and sometimes felt apprehensive when walking my dogs at night but there I was, walking completely alone through the shadowy, narrow back streets of Hiroshima... a town our allies had reduced to a radio-active wasteland only a few years earlier. Curiously... perhaps naively, I felt no threat as I wandered down the dimly-lit alleys.

"Konbanwa, boy-san!" said the elderly lady seated on the porch of the darkened house.

"Konbanwa, Mama-san," I replied. "Anatawa genki desu-ka?"

"Geki pari-pari arigató," she responded to my greeting. "You want short time... all night?"

Suddenly, the reality of my situation hit me... I was alone in a city with absolutely no cause to love me and my kind and good cause to hate us.

"Gomen nasai, Mama-san... habba no yen... no money..."

"For you... purezento!" she said and called sharply into the house.

I realise that memory and imagination lead to exaggeration, but, don't forget, that these circumstances were exceptional.

Down the stairs at the side of the porch came a girl...a child of sixteen... or less, dressed in a cream satin kimono. She was totally unlike the brash, painted bar-girls but delicate, timid and pretty.

"Purezento ... she purezento for you..." repeated the Mama-san.

I'll never know whether it was my inexperience... my fear of the mysteries of sex... some dreadful ambush or the fragile stillness and acceptance of the girl which caused me to mutter a half-embarrassed apology and farewell and set off, my mind whirling, to the normality of Sergeant Parry and three-card brag.

To dispel my wimpish image, I did date one of the very attractive Japanese ladies. She worked in a shop and eventually, I did pluck up enough courage to ask her to go out with me and, to my astonishment, she agreed. I met her, as arranged, when she finished work and asked where she would like to go. We finally decided that we would go to the local cinema but she explained to me that we could not walk together through the streets as to be seen with a soldier meant that her reputation as a 'good girl' would be irrevocably damaged. We walked parallel on opposite sides of the street to the cinema where I paid for her ticket.

We sat, not touching, through a film which consisted of samurai warriors leaping about with razor-sharp swords occasionally screaming and grunting. I was far too conscious of the proximity of my companion to try to translate the screams and grunts into a plot. I do remember that most of the grunters were eventually sliced in half!

When this bewildering cinematic experience was over, we again separated and walked our parallel way to a quiet beer-hall where my date allowed me to buy her a drink before explaining that good girls had to go to bed...alone!

I remember someone of my generation saying that, in his youth, he'd walked many a mile 'on a promise'. For my one and only Japanese 'date' I walked a good stride on less than a promise. I don't know to this day whether I was 'conned' or whether I should have been more assertive. As it was, I decided to cut my losses and chalk it up to lack of experience.

My first visit to a brothel came during my leave in Tokyo. Four of us were window-shopping on one of the main streets when a smart, young, Japanese guy came up to us.

"You want woman, Johnny? Short time... all night... you come see..."

"Fuck off... you're a pimp!" said one of my companions.

The lad was not put off his mission in the slightest. "Yes, me pimp... me honest pimp. Lovely girls... you come... you see..."

By this time, I knew my limitations... however tempting the girls might be, I knew I could not summon up the courage to go through with such a transaction. I tried to persuade the others to forget it but they... *we*... were caught up in the excitement of the exotic setting and the temptations of this apparent sexual license. The young man's description of himself as an 'honest pimp' had caught their fancy and we were off.

We followed the 'honest pimp' through a labyrinth of tiny streets and alleys far from the neon-lit security of the main shopping area. All the time I expected to hear the pounding of feet in pursuit or see a lurking gang spring from ambush but our guide eventually stopped in front of a pleasant house in a quiet back street.

We were ushered into a dim, cool hallway at the front of the house and asked to sit on a bench.

A minute or two later, five or six girls came into the hall and stood facing us, obviously waiting for us to make our choice. My mates had none of my fears and imaginings and quickly disappeared for their short times. They left me sitting wondering which of us had the most sense and feeling decidedly ashamed of my own lack of bravado.

It was in Tokyo also that I encountered the chivalrous Maori giant. The Maoris are a fierce warrior race famed for their leaping about in their short raffia skirts and sticking their tongues out at royalty.

My Maori was big... very big... he was drunk and he was looking for a fight. As we approached the camp gates after a visit to the cinema to see the latest block-buster screening, he called to me; "Hey, you... come here!"

I had no quarrel with Maoris... a fine, Polynesian race and, as I never have been a fan of royalty, the Maoris can stick their tongues out with impunity for my money. Therefore, I approached this coffee-coloured colossus with equanimity.

"Me, mate... what do you want me for?"

"I'm going to knock your fucking head off!" he cried. "I'm going to bash your fucking face in!"

I began to wish that Captain Cook or Van Deimen or whoever had discovered New Zealand had not taken the pretty route through the Antipodes... or chosen a different profession!

It sounds a stupid thing for me to have said but, at the time, it was the only response which sprang to mind. "Why?" I asked.

Peter Flint

"Because you're a fucking, cheating bastard… that's why!" he snarled.

Now, I had never seen this bloke before in my life. Had he been wearing his raffia skirt and leaping about, I might have recalled him but, try as I might, I could think of no previous meeting which could have caused this desire to remodel my face.

"Here, mucker… what's he supposed to have done?" asked one of my mates.

"He's fucked off without paying," said the Kiwi.

Now, I still had the ticket-stub for the cinema somewhere in my pocket and I suspected that even in Japan, threats of extreme physical violence seemed a bit over-the-top for sneaking into the flicks.

"Fucked off where? Paying who? We've been at the fucking pictures all evening… haven't we lads?"

His huge, flat face creased into a puzzled frown as he listened to the counsel for the defence. "She says it was him," he growled, pointing at me. "He's been with her and buggered off without paying… the cheating bastard!"

He indicated a tiny Japanese lady in a jade-green kimono who was looking almost as scared… (notice I said *almost*) …of her Antipodean galahad as I was!

"Can't have been him mate," said my pal. "I've told you... we've all been to the pictures... New film... that new... er... three-D effect... Cinemascope...yeah, that's it...Cinemascope."

By this time two military policemen, both almost as big as my Maori, had arrived on the scene. Gradually, the story came out... In broken English combined with the odd word of Japanese we had all acquired, the M.P.s questioned the bar-girl. It was true that someone had availed himself of her favours and flown the coop and the mighty Maori had sallied forth to right her wrong.

"Why him, girl-san?" asked the M.P. gently, pointing at me.

She indicated the silver buck on my cap-badge... it was her sole means of identifying her vanished ex-client!

"Fuck me," said the M.P. who had become convinced of my innocence. "You were lucky he didn't clock you!" He, too, pointed to my regimental badge. "Royal Warwicks... there must be fucking hundreds of your lads around... could've been any one of 'em!"

This incident gave me a whole new outlook on the expression 'the buck stops here'!

* * *

Did I lose my 'cherry'? This is what you've been asking yourself all through this chapter... isn't it?

Well, it was like this... The beer-hall was crowded as myself and a couple of mates pushed our way through to join another pal of ours at a corner table. We had hardly ordered our beers when a couple of bar-girls came over and sat at our table. We bought them drinks and sat chatting… if a conversation in which the participants only have a few phrases of the others' language, can be described as chatting. We were young and they were pretty… and female… so the language barrier was insignificant.

A few minutes later, the girls chattered excitedly and waved to another girl who had just come into the bar. She came over and sat with us.

She did not look like the typical bar-girl. Her dress and make-up were more discreet and she spoke English, although with a strong Canadian accent. She told us that she had worked for two years at the nearby Canadian base as a secretary but was now working in this bar.

Whether it was the slight 'girl-next-door' image, the lively atmosphere of the bar, the beer or her undoubted attractiveness, I'll never know but suddenly I decided… 'carpe diem'… this was it! The snag was the round of drinks had left me with a serious cash-flow problem. I felt the genie of the wimp stir within me and say, "You've no money, Peter, lad… nobody can blame you if you hang on to your 'cherry for another day."

Deep down, I knew it was now or never… well, now or in some unimaginable future. The words collected in my throat… they formed in my mouth… In just a few seconds it would have been decided and I would have borrowed the necessary cash and the gorgeous ex-secretary would be plucking my cherry as it were.

Just as my lips moved, my mate opposite nodded to the girl and she gathered up her coat and they left together. I sat with a tumbling brain, an open mouth and an unplucked cherry!

Every story should have a happy ending and this one did... at least, for me. My pal who had snatched my beautiful cherry-picker literally from under my nose, was due to sail home a few weeks after the incident I have just described. Sail he did... complete with a certificate from the camp's medical officer which confirmed that he was responding to treatment for V.D.! They say life is just a bowl of cherries but when I heard this, I was glad mine had not turned into one of those nasty, squishy, rotten ones!

Now you know... I never did lose my 'cherry' but, during my year in Japan I certainly learned a great deal about how one went about doing so! Sex was so openly available that inevitably our attitudes changed... and, for some unlucky lads... their equipment was irrevocably altered.

The happy day eventually came and we were on our way home. Once again we threaded our way through Aden's dusty alleys. Again, we were accosted by a grimy urchin... possibly the same one a year older.

"You want woman, Johnny? You come... me show you..."

On the outward journey, Puritanism and disgust had provoked an angry dismissal. This time we all replied to his question with one voice;

"How much?"

Report Document #007

MEET INTERESTING PEOPLE

You'll have seen the ads...

'Join the professionals... learn a trade... travel the world ...meet interesting people... and kill them!'

During my time in the army, thankfully, I never did get round to actually killing anyone. This might seem a terrible waste of tax-payers' money as, after all, that is what I was being trained to do. From purely a personal point of view, I was entirely in favour of Chinese taxpayers wasting their money! I digress... I never did kill anyone but I did travel and I did meet some interesting people...

One of these folk occupied the bed-space next to mine for a brief period. He ate razor-blades and light bulbs! I've heard of a sharp taste and a light diet but I ask you! I cannot recall much about this individual except that he was built like a breeze-block outbuilding and his face looked as if it had at some time lost several rounds with a rotivator!

He came back one night in a violent rage, having consumed more drink than was good for him. Apparently,

Peter Flint

he was nursing a massive grudge against a corporal who had put him on a charge. Stumbling into the next barrack-room, he picked up a mug from a locker, smashed it and stabbed its broken edges into the face of the man lying asleep on the bed.

Not only was his vengeance horrific… he picked the wrong man… a corporal who had played no part in the previous affair!

* * *

'Hard' is an adjective much-used in the teenage macho world of today. Thinking back, I never felt particularly threatened during my army years despite my D.C.M… .'Devout Cowards' Medal'… but some of the characters with whom I lived cheek by jowl (so to speak) would have made many of Britain's current crop of bully-boys seem tame.

I didn't know Perkins very well but I didn't consider him to be a hard case. He was a corporal, a regular soldier who fulfilled some obscure duty in the Quarter Master's Stores or somewhere. Therefore, I felt mild surprise when he appeared in our office, under escort, to collect his personal documents. It transpired that he had been involved in a brawl in town and was on a serious charge.

We later discovered that he had 'rigged' this fight as his brother, in Blighty, had written to him offering him a partnership in a garage he had bought if he could get out of the army. This was easier said than done for he had signed on for more years than I care to think about.

He did not have sufficient money to buy his freedom - this was a legitimate method of reducing the contracted years of service. His brother could not supply the necessary cash, as he needed all his funds for the new business. Ergo... the corporal's only recourse was to be granted a Dishonourable Discharge from Her Majesty's Forces. It was with this in mind that he had somehow engineered the situation in which he now found himself.

In due course, he was court-martialled and sentenced to lose his rank... three months' detention... and a Dishonourable Discharge... Bingo!

A week or so after this happy outcome Captain Warburton, the camp legal officer, strolled into our office and said to Sergeant Parry, "I say, sarn't, can you get out Corporal Perkins' papers for me? I feel he's been given a bit of a raw deal. You know... decent chap before his bit of bother... punishment seems a bit harsh. I'm going to appeal and see if I can't at least get the Dishonourable Discharge quashed."

Another quiet, inoffensive, little chap in the Norfolk Regiment worked in the Motor Pool. Standing only the odd inch or so above five feet, he was a friendly, chirpy, little bloke, always ready for a chat and a joke. I remember the good-natured profanities when he discovered he'd been posted to Singapore - at least it was two stages nearer home!

Like many others, he departed from the camp and was more or less forgotten as we never expected to see him again.

Peter Flint

A few weeks later, we docked in Singapore on our blessed journey home for demob and there he was on the dockside... flanked by two gigantic 'Red Caps'... the army term for military policemen. These M.P.s were ignored as we eagerly greeted our old chum and naturally asked what scrape had caused him to acquire his two forbidding bookends.

He had killed a man in a Singapore bar. He told us the story quite openly with his escort looking on impassively. He had been the regular boyfriend of one of the local bar-girls, sleeping with her two or three times a week taking meals at her place and so on... a common enough situation.

One night, he had come into the bar and found her with another soldier. A quarrel had ensued and he had taken a knife and stabbed his rival to death! He appeared totally unperturbed, unchanged, the same chirpy little character from the J.R.B.D. motor pool.

* * *

Have you ever wondered how the police begin the task of investigating crimes? Of their very nature, most crimes take place away from the openness of day and out of sight of witnesses. I have the greatest respect for police officers facing such a daunting task.

There were, however a couple of occasions when the Military Police's detective skills would have made Inspector Clouseau seem like Sherlock Holmes. Both these occasions involved deserters...

The army makes no pretensions to being kind, comfortable or hospitable but it objects strongly to people leaving without a forwarding address. Thus deserters were assiduously sought... no doubt 'pour encourager les autres'.

It was with some surprise that we learned that the military police were seeking one of our number. Even the least streetwise amongst us could have told them where he was... many could have told them the part of town and some also the name of the little bar-girl with whom he was happily shacked-up.

Some people have fairies at the bottom of their gardens... I had a deserter at the bottom of my bed! He was sitting there drinking a mug of tea I had bought him from the N.A.A.F.I. No doubt the fuzz were scouring the local area for him... perhaps they felt that the barrack-room immediately below where they all slept was not the most likely place for a hideout.

The more astute among you will be thinking that if he was back in camp, he could not, by definition, be a deserter but you are wrong. He regularly crawled under the wire into camp to 'steal' his own kit which he sold to fund his love-life with yet another bar-girl.

A deserter... and a thief! How then was I chatting amicably with such a villain? The lads who deserted, or, as the army had it, went A.W.O.L. (Absent Without Leave) were rarely thugs. They just disliked the army... an attitude which most of us found eminently sensible if not laudable. And as for being a thief? As he was stealing his own kit, our dubious morality was not particularly disturbed.

A tough organisation like the army inevitably had its share of villains… it also had its methods of dealing with them! Hard cases often appeared 'on orders' in front of the company commander with black eyes and/or contusions inevitably caused by their "walking into the edges of doors!" There was an escalating system of punishments ranging from the seven days 'jankers' which I have described, to several years in the 'glasshouse', as the Army Prison was called… not a happy thought!

I only heard rumours of the treatment meted out to offenders in the Field Punishment Centre in Korea but, true or not, they were graphic enough to inhibit any tendency I might have had to buck the system. Solitary confinement in small corrugated iron 'kennels' upon which the duty piquets would beat their pickaxe handles every half hour throughout the night was one of the horror stories which filtered back. I cannot verify these tales which may have been fabrications or exaggerations. I do know that the army's serious criminals were… and had to be… very hard men. However, few, if any, were hard enough to beat the system…

At J.R.B.D., I did briefly meet the only lad that had actually fought in the Korean War… I presume that troops were sent home more directly rather than passing through the camp at Kure when their tour in Korea finished. This lad was convalescing from shrapnel wounds he had received. Reminiscent of W.W., the Chinese were dug in tunnels and elaborate systems of trenches defended their positions on the hilltops. There had been an attack by allied troops and this lad was in one of the tunnels when, from the other direction, came several enemy soldiers. Outnumbered, he turned and ran… one of the Chinese troops threw a grenade and he caught the blast and the shrapnel in his buttocks! I shudder to think what the whole terrifying experience must have been like and, again, have often wondered how I would have coped in similar circumstances.

Whether it was Western propaganda or not we had heard that the weapons the Chinese troops had were of very poor quality and the grenades were made from some sort of heavy-duty plastic… I'll never know the truth of that but, thankfully, this lad survived. Another 'story' was that when the Chinese troops charged many were armed only with flags… or nothing at all! If this is true, it is the same madness that sent young men in the Zulu War to charge and face certain death so that their leaders could pinpoint the British gun positions. Of course, in both these incidents the tactical sacrifices were from backward, primitive FOREIGN people! Oh, I've just remembered, the Scottish piper(s) who, bagpipes skirling, led British troops into battle in W.W.!.

Sadly, I met few Japanese folk… I would have found it difficult to communicate despite the example I have given of my command of their language. We did have a 'human' sergeant in charge of the office for a while… I don't know what happened to Sergeant Parry… still they never did dig up that corner of the sports field… not me, Sir, honest! Despite my obvious bias against N.C.O.s and Officers which, no doubt, you will have noticed by now, were basically decent blokes… (At least the N.C.O.s were…) I never got to meet any of the Officer class. Sgt Thompson was friendly, pleasant and thoughtful. He had a 'lady friend' in Kure and we once went to her home. I can only remember that it was solidly built of wood, spacious and the interior walls of the rooms did have wood and possibly some form of paper screens for walls. The floors, where one sat, were covered with immaculately clean straw or bamboo matting. At the entrance was an idea I have often thought of using and possibly patenting but never got round to… custom decreed that one should take off one's shoes and slippers were laid out near the entrance for guests to wear.

We had a Japanese clerk who worked in our office with Les, Ginger and yours truly. He spoke fluent English and had been a sergeant (or equivalent rank) in the Japanese Army in W.W.II. We had been brought up with the concept that the Japanese were an evil, barbaric race and many were the tales of their horrifying cruelty. There was some truth in this… the treatment of the Allied P.O.W.s was horrendous. The film, starring Alec Guiness… 'Bridge over the River Kwai' gave a graphic account of the suffering enduring in constructing the railway line and the eponymous bridge.

I did have a personal verification of these stories. Two friends and colleagues of mine in the Civil Service, Cliff and Bernard, had both served in the Army in the Far East. Bernard had fought in Burma and Cliff had been taken prisoner by the Japanese after the Allied surrender in Singapore. Bernard used to tease Cliff that while he had been 'up to his neck in mud and bullets' Cliff had been safe and snug in his P.O.W. Camp! This used to shock me but I have since thought that joking about dreadful experiences can, at times, help people to deal with them.

Cliff's experience was by no stretch of the imagination, the 'cushy number' of Bernard's joking. He gave us graphic accounts of some of the bestial treatment the prisoners received and the near-starvation diet they were fed when they had to labour in the sun for hours. He described how, if they caught a snake while they were working, they killed it and, for fear of retribution, hid it coiled round their waist under their shirt. When they got back to camp and were sure they were safe, they would cook and eat it.

Like J.R.B.D., the camp was infested with rats and the Japanese offered a reward of a cigarette to any prisoner who handed into the camp Guard-Room a dead rat. The prisoner had to wait, head bowed, outside the Guardroom, until one of the Japanese came out. Then the prisoner had to bow and hand over the rat. He was then given the cigarette. The Japanese soldier would then dump the rat in the bins at the back of the Guardroom where one of the prisoners would be waiting hidden from sight. When he was sure it was safe, he would retrieve the rat and take it back to the prisoners' hut where it would be cooked and eaten!

I cannot think how we ever got into a discussion of our perceived cruelty of the W.W.II Japanese with our clerk who was now a part of the team, if only peripherally... each day he brought a rectangular tin to work... we did occasionally offer to share our food but the tin contained a dish of meat and cooked rice which he ate with chop-sticks. He told us that, albeit far more extreme, the treatment of Allied P.O.W.s had similarities to the routine diet and the unbelievably harsh discipline in the Japanese Army... he said that, for a minor misdemeanour, the Japanese N.C.O.s and Officers would not hesitate to punch the soldier viciously. I know some of you are thinking, 'Well he would say that wouldn't he?' and I am not excusing the dreadful abuse of the prisoners but it does go a little way to illustrate how the culture might have influenced their treatment. I have also read or heard that their culture decreed that those who surrendered were unworthy cowards and, therefore, not deserving of any sympathy.

* * *

I sat behind a trestle table in the sunshine. A long queue of men stood at ease waiting to see me... they were lads recently arrived from Korea and waiting to be transhipped to other postings. It was my job to check the details of their previous posting and confirm that we had the documentation necessary for their new destinations.

The procedure was routine, boring and frustrating but relaxed and informal. I was, therefore, surprised when before me stood a gleaming, little, ramrod figure. He was immaculate in every detail... his brasses shone... his boots gleamed... his creases would have put razors to shame. His face, staring straight above my head, was impassive and his answers to my questions jerked out in a robotic bark...

"Right," I said, "What's your name, mate?"

"Parrish, staff!" he crackled.

"Number?"

"2784653... staff!"

"Previous posting?"

"223 F.P.C... .staff!"

By this time I was becoming embarrassed, "Hang on mate, there's no need for all this Queen's Regs bullshit you know. I'm only a buck private like you... no need to call me 'staff'."

As far as I was concerned, the poor bastard had done his time and someone who had kicked against the army - or, at least, tried to - could not be all bad. But I was wasting my time... he was like a dog who has been beaten into submission. He was not defiant or snarling... he had learned to respond to any authority figure in a mechanised, respectful manner. I often wondered what harassment and torment had produced this polished automaton and what thoughts of hatred and revenge were going through his mind as he spat answers into the empty air.

* * *

The camp cinema was free. It ran a regular programme of films... perhaps not the latest box-office raves, but, nevertheless, recent and entertaining releases. Every evening Roy would project the magnified ghosts of our heroes... Alan Ladd, Errol Flynn, Gary Cooper, John Wayne... onto the silver screen. On one evening each week, these ghosts did not fret and strut. The screen stayed dark and silent and Roy and his two mates went into town to get drunk.

All three were good lads, typical scousers with quick wits and good-humoured back-chat but we viewed their weekly outings with a mixture of tolerance and irritation. One of the soldier's constant desires is sleep... he will sleep anywhere, any time. Imagine then a darkened barrack-room... murmurs, mutterings, gentle snores...

"One... two... grab! One... two... lift! One... two... tip!"

"What the fuck...!" yelled the corporal from the tangle of bedding on the floor. "Oh, it's you silly cunts again! Do you know what time it is? These lads are trying to get some sleep!"

A slurred, apologetic voice stage-whispered, "Sorreee, lads... sorreee!"

Another voice offered a sort of garbled explanation of why the corporal had been snatched from the arms of Morpheus... or Betty Grable... by being tipped out of his cot.

"This bugger woke us up at five o'clock last week when he was duty corporal, asking if we wanted to buy a battleship!"

"All right... all right you dozy buggers... you've got your own back. Now get to bed... a joke's a joke but fuck a pantomime!" said the corporal who had, indeed, played this well-worn practical joke on the three lads. "Come on, you've had your fun... now let these lads get some sleep..."

In the darkness we heard stifled giggles, snatches of conversation and not-so-muted noises of boots, belts, etc being flung down as they undressed. Eventually... silence!

"Goodnight, corp... only a joke, corp."

"Yes... O.K. lads... no offence... get some sleep."

"Goodnight lads."

A muttered chorus of... "Night!" ... "Fucking stroll on!" ... "Belt up!"... "For fuck's sake" ...and "mine... get your heads down!"

Silence...

"Ten bints were good... weren't they, Roy?"

"Yeah, yeah... great... shurrup... these lads are trying to sleep."

Silence...

"Sorry Roy."

Silence...

"Sorry lads."

"Oh... Jesus wept... settle down."

Silence... then... a frenzied wail...

"Me watch! They've took me watch! Roy, Them bints have got me fucking watch!"

"I've got your watch, Ron. I'll look after it. Go to sleep now, Ron."

Silence...

Thanks, Roy... you're a mucker, Roy. Goodnight, Roy."

"Yes... O.K., Ron... I've got your watch safe. Goodnight, Ron."

Silence...

"You're a good lad, Roy..."

"Yes, alright Ron... now get to sleep."

The silence lasted somewhat longer; then out of the pregnant darkness... a conversational observation. "You know, Roy... I'm a funny bloke about sleeping... I drop off all of a sudden..."

No sooner had this beery, self-analysis been delivered than there was a tremendous crash which shook the room. Ron had indeed 'dropped off'... in his bleary drunkenness, he had fallen out of bed!

There followed a council of war between his two hoppoes...

"Christ... he's fallen out of bed!"

"These blokes'll fucking kill him if he doesn't shut up and let them get some sleep..."

"Let's get him back to bed..."

"That'd no fucking good... in his state, he'll just fall out again.."

"I know... we'll put the mattress on the floor... then he can't fall out..."

"Great! Right come on then..."

There was a grunting and slithering as the mattress was heaved onto the floor. A whispered concert of profanity and reassurance as the recumbent Ron was coaxed onto the mattress.

Silence at last... total blissful tranquillity... for about five minutes! Then we heard... 'boing!'... 'sproing!'... 'bing!'... Boing! You've guessed it... Ron had clambered from his cosy mattress on the floor onto the bare, bedsprings where he slept like a baby until reveille.

* * *

Little and Large they were but, though they were close friends, two more different characters, it was difficult to imagine. Bombardier Flannery was an amiable, giant of a man whose slow, rolling, Devonshire vowels evoked a vision of sunlit meadows and apple-trees. Ratcliffe, his mate, was small, mean-eyed, foul-mouthed and vicious.

Regularly these two would head for the beer-halls in town and, almost inevitably, Ratcliffe would bad-mouth somebody and fists and bottles would fly. We could never understand why such a good-natured bloke as Flannery used his size and strength to rescue time and time again a spiteful mini-shit like Ratcliffe.

It was with some delight that we learned that the two of them had fallen out and were going separately into town. It caused greater delight when the story broke that Ratcliffe, unable to restrain his evil tongue yet without his mate, had made racist remarks about some Maoris… Now, there must be some small Maoris but I never saw any! Those that I did see looked as if they had been destined from birth to lead the New Zealand rugby squad so Ratcliffe, therefore, not only lacked size… he lacked sense! With the inevitability which you knew that the idiot in the saloon would regret purposefully spilling John Wayne's glass of 'red-eye', Ratcliffe got his. He took a severe beating... broken bones and numerous stitches... truly a consummation devoutly to be wished!

It takes all sorts to make up an army and, during my two years in the mob, I met all sorts!

Peter Flint

MY FRIEND ONCE ALMOST DANCED WITH OTTILIE PATTERSON!

Have you ever met anyone really famous? You know… that half-glance of recognition, that hastily swallowed greeting as you realise that you have seen their face on T.V. and that he or she, of course, does not know you from Adam… despite the fact that you are dressed differently from Eve's hubbie!

Since leaving the mob, I have been cheek by jowl… well *almost*… with the Duke of Edinburgh; had an almost personal wave from the Queen too! I have also caught fleeting glimpses of Prince Charles and Lady Diana as they glided past my cheering pupils to various local duties. At a ball in Cambridge, my daughter was burned on the shoulder by the cigar of one of Prince Edward's friends as he was scurrying back to the inner circle. As you can see, in later years I have been inextricably tied up with the highest in the land whereas, at the time of this story, I was entirely excluded from the company of the glitterati.

Peter Flint

During my National Service, this was to change and I was destined to rub shoulders with some famous folk... well, perhaps not quite shoulders...

I was crawling through the soaking grass and mouldering leaves of an Autumn woodland. It was about eight-thirty in the evening, dark and misty. All around me were other creeping figures. Crackles of gunfire and loud explosions sounded nearby. Suddenly, a flare soared into the sky and burst with a crack. As it floated down, the damp, forest floor with its squirming creatures was brilliantly lit.

As instructed, I froze into immobility but, hearing voices directly above me, I glanced up to see a group of officers some six feet away from my prone body. A further glance confirmed that the features gazing down on me with mixed incredulity and apprehension were those of Viscount Montgomery of Alamein! Yes, it was Monty himself... moustache, beret, double cap-badge and all. As our eyes met, I thought, 'Christ! It's Monty!' He no doubt thought, 'Christ! It's Flinty! What chance have we got now of holding back the red communist tide which threatens the world?'

Monty was, in fact, commander-in-chief of our regiment and the following afternoon gave us all a rousing, patriotic speech none of which I remember. All that comes to mind is the incredible, technicolour splash of medal-ribbons which seemed to cover the entire front of his tunic. Later, I exaggerated this tale slightly, saying that he had so many medal-ribbons that his batman had to stand next to him with his second-best B.D. (battle-dress) on a hanger in order to show them all!

You would think it would be difficult to top this close encounter with the very important kind but I did... I met Lassie's stand-in. We had recently arrived in Japan and were having a drink in a beer-hall. Also at the bar were two American sailors. My experience of such exotic creatures was hitherto confined to the movies and I half-expected these two to break into a complicated, tap-dance routine ending with a knee-slide along the bar-counter.

Somewhat nervously, we got into conversation with these two Yanks, mainly about Japan, service life, food, and, of course, home. Then one of them said, "Don't you guys recognise me?"

We obviously didn't so I said, "No... why should we?"

"You've probably seen me in the movies," he said.

I should have asked him who he was and in which films he had appeared, but my sense of humour and the suspicion that our urine was being elongated prevented me.

"Yes," I said, "Now you come to mention it, I do recognise you... I had wondered why Lassie hadn't made any films recently."

I suppose it could have ended up with the traditional bar-fight scene with me doing the obligatory slide along the counter to end up in a cross-eyed daze against the wall. As it was, he muttered some uncomplimentary remark about Limeys and he and his mate slunk out. You know... I've often wondered who he was... I don't think he really was Lassie!

I didn't meet Burt Lancaster, Bing Crosby, Danny Kaye or Bob Hope but all of these came to the American base a mile or so from J.R.B.D. to entertain our gallant boys far from their homeland... Well, *their* gallant boys actually, for although we were very occasionally allowed to penetrate U.S. Base Security to visit the camp cinema where they screened all the latest films - sorry, *movies* - when these international stars appeared either in the flesh or on the silver screen, it was 'up yours' to their friends and allies (us). Shoulder to shoulder our two nations might be, but lepers would probably have more chance of being invited to a U.S. celebrity show than their comrades in arms. In fact the first we knew that these world-famous people had been within a couple of miles of us was when the rumour mill ground out the news a week or so after they'd gone back stateside. So much for our special relationship... perhaps they were just getting their own back for George the Third!

Burt Lancaster did, however, feature in a bizarre episode during my time in Japan. While we were in Hiroshima, we went to a Japanese cinema. This formed the top floor of a large, modern department store and it was showing an American film with Japanese subtitles.

Somewhat nervously, we settled ourselves in our seats before the lights went down. We looked around the vast auditorium to discover that we were the only three Europeans in the entire audience. Imagine our feelings when the lights dimmed and the screen was filled with the image of Burt Lancaster… a Vickers machine-gun clenched Rambo-style under his armpit.

Imagine our feelings when we realised that the aircraft he was blowing out of the sky like so many midges were… yes… you've guessed it… Japanese! Crawling under the seats to the nearest exit was a possible course of action but we realised that the audience seemed to be enjoying Burt's cinematic attempt at genocide more than we were. There's nowt as queer as fowk… neither here nor in Japan!

* * *

Whilst on leave in Tokyo, we were strolling by the moated walls and stately pines surrounding the Imperial Palace, when, like a disturbed ants' nest, hordes of miniaturised policemen appeared as if from nowhere. We strolled on until we were stopped by one of the said policemen. Then, out of the gate swept an escort of motor-cycle cops with leather jackets, helmets and sun-glasses for all the world like those on American T.V. Behind them came two large, black cars from one of which, giving us a slight half-wave, peered the Emperor of Japan… Hirohito himself!

* * *

Peter Flint

I must be one of the few people to have been arrested by Gene Kelly... yes, that's right, that Gene Kelly! The arrest took place at the start of the eponymous 'Singing in the Rain' sequence. The love-sick Kelly was just beginning to smile that sickly grimace prior to slopping and splashing his way through a rain-storm which would have had Noah rushing down to the nearest builders' merchants.

He had just begun... "Dum...dee...dee...dum... dum...dee...dum... dee...dee...dum...dum..." when he stopped in mid splosh and said, "Private Flint, Private Hunter and Private Higgins go to the rear of the theatre... you are under arrest!"

Gene repeated this message then got on with his slopping and dumming dance routine as if nothing had happened. I am sure that there are Japanese grandads and grandmas who teach their offspring this song as if our being nicked were part of the lyrics...

Why, I am sure you are asking, did Kelly interrupt one of the best-known film sequences of all time to nick myself and my two buddies?"

Our office was called the Documents Office and, as the name suggests, we processed all the documentation of troops moving into or out of Japan. When a troopship arrived carrying several hundred men, we were very busy for several days. Rarely did we see our beds until two a.m. and, during such a period of hectic activity, our recreation was limited to a hurried mug of tea at the N.A.A.F.I. At this particular juncture, three such boats had docked one after the other and in army parlance 'our feet had not touched the ground'.

Working from early morning well into the night under Sergeant Parry's gimlet eye and biting tongue was no picnic... office workers of today are 'stressed' if their latte is cold. Our weariness and frustration was not soothed when every evening at about seven, Parry would detail the mass of work we had to complete in the next four... five... six... hours then slope off to the Sergeants' Mess to drink with his mates.

When 'Singing in the Rain' was featured at the local Japanese cinema, our cup of misery 'ranneth over'. It was a film we were all desperate to see - the latest Hollywood blockbuster - and there we were stuck in the office! Again, Parry gave his orders and set off for the Mess and our mutinous thoughts seethed over.

To be truthful, ours was a muted mutiny... Captain Bligh probably wouldn't even have noticed it. Not for us the glamour and danger of escaping our confinement with a swashbuckling laugh to rush to the arms of our oriental doxies. No, we were going to sneak out to the pictures like Meredith of the Remove and be back in the prep room before that beast Quelch... or rather... Parry, caught us and we were 'gated'!

Unless we had actually deserted there was no way that we could avoid doing the work so we devised a plan. We felt that we had earned a break so decided we would see the film, getting back to camp on the last bus about eleven.

Peter Flint

We had left all the work laid out and calculated that we could clear it before four a.m. and get a few hours kip before starting again.

Alas, 'the best laid plans gan Plymouth Argyll…' as Bobby Burns said. For once, Parry decided to leave his boozy N.C.O. buddies and check up on us. He must have enquired in the N.A.A.F.I. where we had gone; grabbed a jeep and come after us!

By an unlucky and amazing coincidence, his Japanese brother-in-law owned the cinema where Kelly… or his shade… was performing and we were watching. The voice we heard emanating from the silver screen was not that of the famous Hollywood hoofer splashing out his saturated love song, but Parry!

As we assembled on the pavement outside the theatre, he barked, "In the jeep… you're under close arrest!"

During the silent, tense twenty minutes drive back to camp the hatred in the vehicle was palpable. Later we each confessed to the same murderous / suicidal thoughts of grabbing the steering wheel and dumping the evil, little bastard in the roadside ditch. There was, however, a snag to this otherwise attractive scenario which you will no doubt have spotted!

Another less spectacular and painful face-saving sequence also crossed our minds. He'd probably get us a week's jankers but he would have to explain to his superiors why the boat had sailed without the necessary documents being on board. I'll explain… you see that while you are under 'close arrest' you cannot, under Queen's Regulations, be compelled to do any work other than keeping yourself and your cell clean and tidy.

We had, however, reckoned without Parry, who, remember had been in the army since Pontius was a pilot… O.K. that's the Air Force but you get my point. As we passed under the J.R.B.D. sign at the camp gate he said, "Now you are under open arrest!"… the bastard!

This episode did end rather like a jolly jape in the dorm story for the anticlimax was that we weren't even formally charged. We were hauled before the Chief Clerk, a Company Sergeant Major, who heard our story… gave us a rollocking and sent us on our way… we had worked until all hours to clear the work. I've a feeling that he was a decent bloke who hadn't any more time for Parry and his bullying tactics than we had.

I did see the complete unabridged version of 'Singing in the Rain' again… innumerable times! It is still one of my all-time favourite films but every time Gene Kelly smiles that sickly smile and begins humming, 'Dum…dee…dum…dum… dum…dee…dum…dee…dum…dee…' I anticipate an arresting performance!

Peter Flint

Report Document #009

BE A SPORT!

If you had played First Division football or boxed in the A.B.A. Championships, army life was a doddle. Not for you the remorseless square-bashing and tedious shining and polishing… you were to be groomed for stardom. The ability of the Charlie Company soccer, rugby or rifle-shooting team to humiliate their rivals of the Fifty-Fourth Foot and Mouth was of paramount importance in the army's higher echelons.

Sadly for me, any sport involving extraneous equipment, for example… a ball… a racquet… a gun… was doomed to total failure. I was always the last one to be picked when our gang of urchins made up a football team and then at times only if they had insufficient coats to represent the goalposts.

However, I could run several miles across muddy fields and icy roads with a fair turn of speed. Although any sporting ability was admired by the army, my running did not elevate me to the pampered-pets league… perhaps being able to run quickly is not such a desirable military asset. Nevertheless, I did achieve one or two minor sporting successes.

Peter Flint

We were training in Budbrooke Barracks in Warwick and my company was getting psyched up by the P.T.Is (Physical Training Instructors) to win the inter-company cross-country race. It was a beautiful day for the said race... crisp, cold but sunny. A blue sky contrasted with the brazen glory of the distant woods.

"On your marks... get set... go!"

Away we pounded some eighty of us and I was revelling in the exhileration of the clear air and the physical effort. Within a mile I was shoulder to shoulder with a ginger-haired youth with whom I was sharing the lead. Feeling good, I stepped on the gas a little and he fell back.

As I approached the first P.T.I. who was acting as a course steward there was no one in sight behind me.

"Christ... you've been moving!" he said.

"Which way, corp?" I panted, jigging briefly on the spot.

"Go diagonally across the race-course that way and you'll find an alley... follow that and you'll come to a path leading to barracks."

Off I went across the springy turf of Warwick Race-Course. As indicated by the corporal, I climbed over a stile and found, as he had said, a footpath. I felt full of running... no one was even insight behind me... I had the race won! I turned onto the main road paralleling the wall of the barracks... half a mile or so and it was in the bag!

I glanced over to my left only to see, to my horror, a long line of plodding figures at the base of the barracks' wall. Then I realised... I had found a path alright but it was the wrong one! The route I had taken added at least a mile to the cross-country course and now, instead of trotting in a glorious but modest winner, I was to finish a disappointed forty-second or thereabouts.

Army tradition tended to bounce off most of we National Service soldiers like water off the proverbial duck's back. The bullshit engendered to commemorate some minor skirmish on the Khyber Pass in eighteen-hundred and umpty-bleep or the stiff upper lip and tight sphincter needed while trying to unjam the Gatling in the Zulu Wars was, for us, singularly lacking in glamour.

Battalion Day was no exception... lots of bull... shouting and aimless marching hither and yon was an inevitable traditional ingredient. True to the concept of keeping the rough soldiery physically active and mentally torpid, the afternoon of Battalion Day was to be devoted to sport.

If you are imagining egg and spoon races, three-legged sprints, sack-races or chucking the welly, forget it. The format was simple... each of the companies would field its glamour-boys... the company soccer team. The rest would run in a six and a half mile cross-country race across the Downs... these were, in fact, not Downs but Ups!

Peter Flint

Minus the footballers, about twelve hundred men, including, to his credit, the C.O., massed on the parade-ground. A blast on the bugle and away we surged...

In my Grammar School cross-country team, pacing oneself and packing were constantly preached. This meant that one was supposed to set off steadily thus conserving energy and also run as far as possible with team-mates... this latter was known as 'packing'. I was beginning to discover the flaws in this seemingly sound strategy... when it came time to unleash the conserved, pent-up energy, the opposition was usually so far ahead that the effort was futile. I was realising that if one intended to feature, one had to get near the front early on and stay there.

As we came out of the main gates of the camp in a panting flood, I was lying fourth. Feeling O.K., I increased my pace and found myself in the lead. Few runners like to lead early in the race and I was no exception but I pressed on, gradually leaving the mass behind. Through the checkpoints I went where some ingenious person had hit on the idea of rubber-stamping our upper arms with the camp's 'Top Secret' stamps thus ensuring that we had, in fact, completed the whole course.

Over the final crest I came, still leading, only to find a nasty, strung-wire fence. As I negotiated this obstacle I saw another runner who was either more nimble than I was or had found an easier section of the barrier for he was now five or six yards in front of me. At first I was tempted to give in and settle for second place but I thought, 'I've come this far... I'm not going to let this bugger beat me!' I increased my speed and came up level with him as we entered the final stretch... the eight hundred yard firing range.

Neck and neck we pounded down the length of the range. One by one the firing points at each hundred yard interval slipped behind us... Four hundred... three hundred... two hundred... we were sprinting now and he was still there. One hundred... an open patch of grass... and a huddle of figures standing on the finishing line... Suddenly, I was aware that he'd gone... he had faded back and I'd won! I was the Battalion Cross-Country Champion!

Some time later I shuffled modestly forward to receive the congratulations of the C.O. and receive my prize from the Colonel's Lady. She smiled graciously: shook my hand and presented me with my prize... a carton of two hundred cigarettes! They obviously did not intend anyone winning the race twice! Ridiculous as the award was... especially to a non-smoker such as myself... it was not unwelcome.

* * *

Every night a bizarre game of musical chairs took place in the huge N.A.A.F.I. canteen. The chairs were ranged around three sides of the large room and those lads waiting interminably to be served hutched their way from chair to chair until they neared the counter. Among this Mexican Wave of potential customers there were always some lads just trying to buy smokes. My prize two-hundred pack disappeared much quicker than my sprint down the firing range and I was richer by half a week's pay. Shamateurism? Perhaps I should have got myself an agent!

When a similar race was organised for the troops in J.R.B.D. camp across the surrounding hills and paddy-fields, word had spread and I was hot favourite to win. Even Sergeant Parry who was permanently antipathetic to my intestines was beaming at me and being matey.

His matey-ness did not last long for I was out of training, unfit and slow... I trailed in shamefacedly well down the field, feeling mentally and physically awful.

This debacle made me determined to get fit and I trained regularly over the fields and on the camp's track. I won the ten thousand metres and the five thousand metre in a match against the Australians and the Kiwis. As a result of these successes, I was thrilled to be chosen to represent the joint Commonwealth Forces team against the Osaka Prefecture... the second strongest athletic association in Japan.

I'd like to say that I was the hero of the hour, winning my race in record time but, alas, it was not to be. Fearing another dismal performance, I went to the other extreme and trained hard every spare minute but the day before the race I felt very ill and went sick. The M.O. diagnosed heatstroke and prescribed rest and salt tablets... the Company Sergeant Major gracefully allowed me to take the salt tablets but he was not so keen on the resting part of the cure!

That day we were to have a mock-disaster exercise... well, it's no good waiting for a proper disaster to descend then wondering, 'Whoops... an earthquake/food/tsunami... what shall I do?' With a pounding head and jelly limbs, I felt as if I was hosting my own personal disaster. To add insult to injury, I was detailed to become a stretcher-bearer and spent the day tearing around in the hot sun loading and carrying healthy, great, grinning squaddies whose arms bore labels indicating their horrific but totally imaginary, injuries.

As if this was not enough, when this exercise finished I was duty-clerk. This was not a particularly onerous task merely involving sleeping on a folding camp-bed in the Orderly Room and answering rare phone-calls or queries. On this evening the enthusiasts who produced the camp newspaper were 'going to press' or 'putting the paper to bed' or whatever journalistic process was required.

At any rate, they were clanging and churning the handle of a primitive copying machine some three feet from my prone body and throbbing temples until gone two in the morning. As you can imagine, I slept little... if at all... and woke feeling as it I'd been dead for several days and no one had bothered to tell me. I looked awful... I felt awful... my pyjamas were soaked in sweat and I was representing the British Commonwealth of Nations in a ten thousand metre race, that evening.

I should have cried off but I was so keen to take this big chance that I half convinced myself that I would feel better. In fact, I did improve but not enough to enable me to give my best performance.

The Japanese team were good! They were dedicated, technically perfect and their team included a number of the country's top athletes, including several Olympic trialists. A good example of their team's ability was in the discus event. Throwing for us was a Canadian major... literally a giant. He was a huge, ginger, freckled mountain of muscle and must have been tremendously strong. He hurled the discus an immense distance through sheer body mass and bull strength.

The Japanese discus thrower, though stocky and well-muscled, was a good eighteen inches shorter than our man... it seemed that he had absolutely no chance. He spun around the discus circle light as a ballet-dancer... his technique was a joy to watch. Every ounce of strength and timing co-ordinated exactly to send the discus flying yards into the lead.

I felt better but not good when my race was called. My partner, the team's first string, was a dour Scot... yes, it's a cliché but, in this case, it was accurate. He hardly spoke to me as we drove to the athletics meeting, nor when we were changing and warming up. I knew that he was a very good runner having run the mile professionally at the famous Meadowbank Stadium in Glasgow... at the time, there was no professional athletics in England... no appearance fee or sponsorship deals. His time had been a few seconds over four minutes... not great by today's standards but, remember, that in Japan I watched a newsreel report of Roger Bannister's world record event when he broke both the four minute mile and the previous world record of four minutes, fourteen seconds! Dour he may have been, but, on the running-track, Jock was no slouch!

Our opposition in the ten thousand metres race was Tanaka... an Olympics trialist... who had already wiped out our lads in the eight hundred and fifteen hundred metres races without breaking sweat. Bearing this in mind, I worked out a plan... I realised that, feeling as I did, I was not going to be able to do much but figured that the Japanese lad would be pretty tired after two hard races. I decided to take the lead from the start and force the pace for as long as I could, hopefully taking some steam out of the formidable Tanaka and leaving my Scottish team-mate to come through to win.

The course was twelve and three quarters laps and from the gun I went off like a rocket. Surprisingly, I did not feel too bad and kept up a fast pace lap after lap. I could sense that someone was just behind me and hoped that it was Tanaka and that he was becoming tan-knackered!

The sizeable crowd were excited to see me pounding along in front. I felt relaxed and calm - the plan seemed to be working although I knew that I could not sustain that pace until the end. One Aussie yelled, "Good on yer... you

Pommie bastard!" which, in case you misunderstood was an Antipodean compliment!

Almost eight laps I held the lead then, as if a tap had been turned, all the strength drained from my legs. I felt heavy and sluggish; I struggled to maintain speed for a further half lap or so. I heard footsteps pattering behind me and Tanaka swept past as if I'd been walking. A moment or two later, the Scot came past and then the young Japanese second string. I plodded on to the finish.

I expect that many in the crowd felt that I had let them down but I had no such thoughts. I had done my best in the circumstances... I had run for the team... my plan might have worked and given us the race. I would have loved to have been fit and given Tanaka and the dour Scot a run... win or lose... but that was not how it worked out.

* * *

There was no ominous music... no underwater shots of myriads of bubbles rising to the surface when I met... Jaws! A group of us occasionally used to walk the mile or so over the hill to a small, secluded bay where, greatly daring for those days, we would swim naked.

Although I love swimming, I have never been one of those folk who jump, splash, leap and cavort in the water. My idea of swimming was to set myself a goal and steadily plough up and down until this target was achieved. On this occasion, I had decided to swim between the two headlands which formed the furthermost points of the bay. My mates were sunbathing; playing football or racing about on the beach.

Backwards and forwards I churned, turning as I touched the algae-covered rocks. I became absorbed with the effort of swimming strongly yet steadily, calculating the distance between the arms of the bay and multiplying it by the number of crossings I had made.

Occasionally, I would look towards the beach which, from my half-submerged position an inch or two above the waves, seemed an incredibly long way off. It immediately appeared much further when I saw my mates yelling and leaping frantically up and down... arms waving... willies jiggling violently. It dawned on me that this frantic semaphore and shouting was directed at me! Then I realised that they were pointing out to sea and I turned my head to see what was the cause of this bizarre pantomime. Then... to my horror... I realised that they were all screaming... "SHARK!"

When telling this tale I always say that I was still thrashing my arms and legs in a manic swimming motion twenty feet up the sand. While that is not strictly true, I can assure you that I've never swum faster... before or since!

What is true is that about a hundred yards off shore, was an unmistakeable triangular fin! I was convinced that it was nothing more than a porpoise... perhaps that's what I really wanted it to be. I am eternally grateful that I never got close enough to it to check!

Peter Flint

Grandad's Army

Report Document #010

NOT WITH A BANG!

My stay in Japan ended abruptly. I had borrowed a bow and arrows and was practising my toxophilic skills when I was summoned to the Orderly Room.

"Just had a radio message from J.R.B.D. in Kure," said the company clerk. "You're to get straight back... you're going home on the next boat."

I was on leave... I had sunlight on the sand... I had moonlight on the sea... I had volleyball and archery... and it was all for free! Funny, I've heard something like that before somewhere... Now I would have hesitated... not that I had much choice in the matter... there was so much of Japan I'd not seen, so much left to do in that beautiful country. However, all I felt when I got this message was delight... every National Serviceman counted the days to going home. Some even had improvised calendars above their beds on which they crossed off each day up to that longed-for 'early breakfast'.

Before the powers that be could change their military minds, I had packed my kit; collected my travel warrant and was on my way back to Kure.

Peter Flint

Most of the lads leaving the Far-East had a strong metal-bound trunk made in Kure. They drew out some of their 'credits'... army savings... to fill the said trunk with: 'satin' embroidered jackets, enamelled boxes, ornate tea-services resplendent with dragons and temples. I had expected to be in Japan for almost another month so my present buying was a frantic affair.

My final farewell party was a big mistake. I was virtually skint after my hurried search for gifts and had little or no cash for a parting binge. Fortunately... or unfortunately as it turned out... my pal, Brian Jakeman, had won five pound in the camp's weekly lottery... Bingo! Doesn't sound much for a boozy rave-up... does it? In those far-off days, five pounds was three weeks wages... a veritable fortune!

In those days, having a drink was not part of the 'out with the lads, let's get legless' culture which seems to have developed. Each week when we went into Kure town, we would do a mini-tour of some of the more obscure bars but rarely did we drink more than two or three beers. On this celebratory occasion we 'let down our hair' and got pretty plastered on the two drinks which were cheap... beer and port wine... they say 'never mix the grape and the grain'... we did and it was a lethal combination! We 'let down our hair' but for the next three days I brought up my stomach ... at regular intervals!

Nor was it helped when I stood or sat in interminable queues to hand in items of kit or, in equally interminable queues to draw out other items! For almost a year I could envisage no more beautiful sight than the ship which would carry me home. When I first saw it rolling like a plastic duck in a Jacuzzi in Kure harbour which was as smooth as a mill pond, my stomach again had the same symptoms of a high-speed lift.

Three days it lurched and reeled over the waves… and the boat was not too steady either. However, nothing could diminish the miracle of actually heading for home and I soon got my sea-legs and what was left of my stomach. Some were not as fortunate… one lad who had been ill the whole voyage, was still being cruelly taunted with offers of greasy bacon sandwiches and similar stomach-turning food as we were sailing through the Med four weeks after setting off.

I too can remember racing down the mess-deck with a tray of fried breakfast held at arm's length because, though I knew I had to eat something or I would feel worse (if that were possible) I could not bear to look at the food. I also recall that the ever-thoughtful army caterers stopped serving mugs of tea as soon as we crossed the line into a warmer latitude, and served mugs of 'lemonade'. This was supposedly more refreshing but was made by pouring water on a hundred-weight of sulphuric acid crystals. I well remember sitting with a huge mug of this potion before me watching the view from the window of the mess-hall oscillating from grey, foam-flecked sea to grey, cloud-flecked sky. I still felt sick but very thirsty… I would actually have been better just feeling sick for, as the bile-green fluid hit the bottom of my stomach, I hit the companion-way running to seek fresh air and to unload this vile-tasting concoction... and the rest of the contents of my stomach... over the ship's rail.

Unlike yours truly, none of the throng packed onto the troopship had their own stateroom. Possibly because of my experience in the Documents Office in J.R.B.D., I was detailed as clerk to the ship's entertainments officer. As his idea of 'entertainment' for the rough soldiers consisted of just two words... 'Bingo' and 'Sing-Song' (is that three words?) my clerical duties were extremely light.

What's more, I did have an office... small but clean and private. This office... my office... had a chair and a desk. The desk was not much used for paper-work but it was big enough to stretch out on and made a solid but excellent bed. While the ship ploughed through the baking heat of the Middle East and the other squaddies climbed desperately out of the stifling tomb of the troop-deck to spread their blankets under the stars on the hard wooden boards, I spread mine on the desk-top and slept the sleep of the truly deserving.

My officer... one that sets the archetypal master/servant roles firmly in place... lacked drive and imagination. In fact, he was a typical member of his class. He would meander into the office with the week's entertainment schedule for me to type and post on the notice boards in the mess and the dining-hall. The programme alternated

Bingo and Sing-Song throughout the five week voyage. I lie... in fact, once each week there was a Talent Contest, one of which I won.

Although petrified with stage-fright, I was, at the time, able to do fair impressions of some of the better-known stars of that era. I could also remember word for word the script of the popular police series 'Dragnet'. Unfortunately, for me... and the audience... my terror at performing in front of several hundred cheering (jeering?) soldiers destroyed the little ability I possessed for singing. I did, however, stagger through a couple of vocal impressions which caused my accompanist... yet another dour Scot... to ask, "Which fucking key were yez supposed tae be fucking singing in?"

I didn't tell him... I had no idea!

Despite his lack of appreciation, I did win the talent contest that week and envisaged a glittering career in showbiz but the two bottles of beer which was my prize were to be the only reward my untapped talent ever received.

The journey passed pleasantly but slowly... writing long letters to my girl-friend back home; sunbathing on the deck; drinking tea and telling jokes in the canteen.

I made sure I was a good boy this time and got shore leave in both Hong-Kong and Singapore. I recall the ferries, like skittering water-beetles, the elegant sails of the Chinese junks, the steep ride on the funicular

Peter Flint

railway to look down on the city and out to the hills of communist China. The China Balm Garden was a cross between Disney and Modern Art with its statues of legendary figures. Above all I recall the excitement of the exotic bustle of the narrow streets and hurrying people.

Each day we entered in the ship's mileage competition and each day the line inched nearer and nearer to home. Now seasoned sailors, we crossed the Bay of Biscay on the return trip without incident and soon crowded the rails for the first glimpse of the Devon coast. Less than a day's sailing and we would be on the train heading north to meet up with old mates… enjoy mum's home cooking and the eagerly awaited first meeting with the girl of whom you'd dreamed all those lonely Spartan nights.

The army, as usual, had other ideas… for over a day and a half we steamed… or 'oiled'… back and forth off Falmouth on sea-trials. As if five weeks and twelve-thousand miles of wind and waves was not enough to check whether the boat was sea-worthy! Finally, we entered Southampton Water passing the grey bulk of naval vessels and the scatter of small boats like leaves on a pond.

Disembarkation… long lines of khaki-clad, grinning, young men descending the gangplank to mill around in a huge shed waiting!

Waiting for what?

Rumours flew round like a swarm of mosquitoes... the train to London was delayed... we each had to be checked through customs. The story spread of one lad who, on hearing of the customs check, threw a kitbag filled with cigarettes into the sea rather than get caught.

At last we clattered aboard the train and were off heading for London, Derby and home!

* * *

The Anglo Saxon word for sexual intercourse is commonplace in today's conversations. It edged its way into near-acceptance by series of subterfuges... blank spaces, the letter 'f' followed by four asterisks, 'chuffing', 'bonking' et al. In 1954 it was very naughty to say or write 'fuck' and you could actually be arrested for using 'foul language'. In the army we didn't give a XXXX for civilian sensibilities and every squaddie's speech was sprinkled liberally with asterisks.

The three of us were no fucking... oops... were no exception but before return to civvie street we decide to embark on a 'no fucking' campaign... conversationally at least. Every time one of us said, "abso... fucking... lutely" or "im... fucking... possible" the others reminded him forcibly!

The plan was working and we were beginning to feel that we would manage to pass as civilians with a bit more... fu... sorry... practice. We eagerly boarded the train which was to take us to the Sherwood Foresters Barracks in Derby where we were to be demobbed. We settled ourselves in the railway carriage and waited for the guard's whistle.

You won't believe this... you will think that I am creating a situation for dramatic tension or perhaps you'll just thing that I'm a bloody liar but it is true. As we sat there picking our way hesitantly through the minefield of conversational rehabilitation, the carriage door opened and in came two priests - dog collars and all!

Didn't we do well... nary a slip for well over half an hour until one of the clergymen asked if we were regular soldiers or doing our National Service. We explained that we had been in Japan for almost a year and that we were on our way to be demobbed. He asked if we had enjoyed our two years in the army and received polite noncommittal responses. Then he asked if we were considering signing on for further military service...

I do not remember which of the three almost-ex-musketeers it was who yelled, "Sign on? Not fucking likely, padre!"

* * *

The five-tonner picked us up at Derby station and bumped and rattled us through an Autumn Saturday afternoon to the Sherwood Foresters' barracks. If we were expecting bands or banners we were unlucky for the place was like the Marie Celeste. The Orderly Room and the Duty Officer's office were as empty as Mother Hubbard's fridge. We weren't particularly surprised... two years in the mob had accustomed us to the 'hurry up and wait!' method of military organisation. We knew that we were, at last, home and it felt good. We knew that before long we would stumble across someone who organised for us; a meal, a bed and a forty-eight hour pass so we set off unhurriedly to find him.

From a long, one-storey building on the far side of the parade-ground we could hear the sound of rifle fire. Here was a good place to begin our enquiries. We entered the rifle-range for one of the most rewarding experiences of my life... certainly up to that point. A sergeant was in charge of a painfully new intake. Their uniforms all looking at least two sizes too large appeared to have been hastily run up using the nasty, hairier type of carpet and their enormous berets stood out as stiff and sharp as Boudiccea's hubcaps. In contrast, we swaggered in tanned from our five weeks' cruise, berets rakishly perched, badges gleaming, creases razor-sharp and weighted, boots sparkling and badges and medal-ribbons proclaiming us as veterans.

"Now then, sarge... only two more days and an early breakfast and that's our lot!"

The awe and admiration in the eyes of the recruits as we swapped stories, acronyms and profane banter with the sergeant who, to them, would be the nearest thing to god for the next nine weeks, almost made the previous two years seem worthwhile... almost!

* * *

Peter Flint

I was strutting up Heanor Road in Ilkeston, my home town, kitbag slung airily over one shoulder, suitcase filled with my exotic presents swinging lightly in my other hand when I heard the roar of a motor-bike which throttled back and stopped alongside me.

"Gully! Didn't expect you this soon. When did you get home then? Eh, are we out tonight?"

It was Pete Watson, a pal of mine who had gone into the R.A.F. at almost the same time as I went into the army and had been demobbed a week or so earlier. Both Pete and I had been pretty good at languages at the Grammar School and he had been singled out to go on an exclusive course learning Russian. There were only twelve National Servicemen chosen for this elite group each year.

They knew no Russian when they joined the services but, by the end of the intensive course, they were fluent. Pete spent the last few weeks of his National Service monitoring Russian military aircraft. I used to joke that the jammy bugger had spent half as much time doing anything remotely useful as I had spent on two fu... blooming boats!

As I have explained, both Pete and I were pretty good at languages at our Grammar School but he was the one, (lucky bugger), who got onto the Russian Course. We used to write to each other... real Snail-Mail letters on parchment and written with quill pens... no mobile phones, text messages and the myriad means of modern communication. Telephones were only used rarely and the vast majority of folk had to walk to the red telephone box on the corner of the street to make a call. As usual, I digress... Russian is a phonetic language which means that it is possible... with effort in my case... to write in English using the Russian Cyrillic alphabet. Pete and I had a daft joke that we wrote the first page of our letters to each other in Cyrillic. I often wondered what the M.O.D. security blokes would have made of two National Service men apparently communicating in Russian at the height of the Cold War!

Pete told me a wonderful story of when his Russian teacher gave them an essay to write in Russian. The title was... 'How to Kidnap a General'... appropriate eh? Pete didn't know the word 'to kidnap' so he looked it up... no not on-line... in one of those paper book thingies called a Russian Language Dictionary. When the teacher handed back the essays he said, "Yours was an excellent essay, Mr Watson... pity about the title... 'How to Rape a General'". Pete had found a word which meant 'to take by force'!

Pete joined the R.A.F. knowing not a single word of Russian... he spent the last five or six weeks of his National Service monitoring the radio messages of Russian military aircraft! After we were both reincarnated as civilians, I used to pull his leg saying, "You jammy, lazy bugger... talk about a cushy number... I spent more time on a bloody boat than you did defending the realm!"

Peter Flint

We had one of those plans... you know... 'I'm going on a diet'... 'I intend to take more exercise' etc... Ours was that Pete and his wife would come round to our house for a meal once a week and Pete would teach me to speak a bit of Russian... the plan lasted about a fortnight! I still know a few Russian phrases... we went out for a meal a few years ago and I learned that the waitress was a Russian girl... she was impressed when I greeted her and thanked her in fluent(ish) Russian. She was, more impressed, when I said, "Ya lubluvas moya dorogaya!" (I'm not sure how it is spelt)... it means, "I love you my darling"... at least I hope so, perhaps Pete had been getting his revenge for my 'lazy bugger' teasing!

Many years after our demob Pete told me that he had a Russian come to his home to visit and the guy arrived with, among other things, a loaf of black bread! No, it wasn't a Russian tradition... he had been led to believe that all British people were desperately short of food, presumably because of our evil Capatalist political system... imagine how his eyes popped when Pete took him to the local supermarket!

Include these anecdotes if you wish. At the end of the 'Land of the Rising...' it might be an idea to add...

I learned much later that Alan Bennett had also been one of the chosen few and wrote to him to ask if, by chance, he and Pete had been in the same intake. I got a nice letter back saying that they hadn't met. The top two in early tests of the group were sent to Oxford for the rest of their service, wearing civvies and, to all intents and purposes, were actually civilians. Alan Bennett had been such a one but Pete, although he came second in his test, for some reason was not given this special treatment.

Where was I? Oh yes… on my final leg to normality…

"Come on, hop on the bike and we'll get you home… bet you're keen to get back, eh?"

I clambered onto the pillion, somehow balancing my luggage between the two of us and, with a fez which I'd bought in Cairo, on my head, we roared homewards.

Cheerfully and noisily, I burst in through the door to number 21, Boweswell Road lugging my case and my kitbag. Immediately I sensed that something was wrong… Mum and Dad had faces set like stone… the room prickled with tension. My elation seeped out like air from a punctured tyre. Pete shuffled uneasily; muttered something about seeing me later and left. The chill 'football-result' hiatus of a dull Saturday evening brought me hurtling down to reality.

"Oh, it's you," said my mother in a brittle voice. "Do you want a cup of tea?"

Recently, I have not been able to resist contrasting this less-than-ecstatic home-coming with the welcoming crowds, the marching through the town, the newsreel footage of smiling, hugging women-folk waiting for the returning soldiers. I realise this sounds a bit churlish and I do not for one moment begrudge those lads their short time

Peter Flint

in the spotlight. They have been in a shooting war while I, thank the lord, just missed one!

IN THE EVENT OF A NUCLEAR ATTACK... STICK YOUR HEAD IN ... ER ... A PRIVATE PLACE... THEN PRAY!

After my riotous homecoming, that should have been the end of my army experience but not quite. We were required after demobilisation to serve two further years in the Territorial Army... as it turned out, this was proving too costly so it was abandoned after my first year in the T.A. This part-time soldiering consisted of attending three weekend camps each year and a fortnight's intensive training in the summer. On second thoughts... perhaps they didn't really abandon it... just renamed it the Open University!

Needless to say, we resented being dragged back into the army even for a few days each year. Our Company Commander in the T.A. was a podgy, ginger insurance salesman called Major Smith. Only the military rank distinguished this pompous prick from the awful mediocrity of everything else about him. He was one of those people who were born a generation too soon to be yuppies. He actually enjoyed playing soldiers at the weekend... even today, executives can dress up in mock

Peter Flint

combat gear and play games in the woods... they call it 'team-building'!

Proteus Camp in North Nottinghamshire was not exactly the Mansfield Hilton, consisting as it did of a collection of whitewashed huts in the middle of open fields, miles from the nearest pub, cinema or coffee-bar. However, it had at least stoves, beds and somewhere to brew up. You can imagine our unrestrained delight when we tumbled off the lorries with our kit and were told by Major Pra... Smith that he had been given the choice of staying in these huts or two-man bivouac tents! Guess which one he had chosen...

Wrong! You have forgotten that (a) he was an army officer and (b) even worse... he was only playing at being one in his spare time. Still, this was his regular macho break from indemnity clauses and growth rate percentages. Add to this the fact that he was a great, fat pillock and guess again. Right! He, of course picked the chuffing tents didn't he?

I was not best pleased when I was sitting on the damp grass of a dreary Nottinghamshire field when I could have been snuggled up with my girlfriend on the back row at the pictures. Having seen Hiroshima and the evidence of the devastation that a relatively small atomic weapon could wreak, I was even less pleased when he started to give us Army Lecture D/47/BL/sub-section 9 A... on how to react when threatened by battlefield nuclear weapons. I didn't actually fall about laughing but I must have conveyed... even to Major Smith... that any reaction, other than that which I have suggested in the title of this chapter, was completely ludicrous.

In any event, he was visibly annoyed at my display of cynicism and, seeing my medal-ribbon, said, "I'm surprised at you soldier! You've obviously seen combat so you know how vital it is to be prepared."

He did not lie: I had indeed seen combat: not for nothing was my medal called The Butcher's Apron or The N.A.A.F.I. medal... some of those queues could be murderous!

I spent my twenty-first birthday in Scarborough doing my first two-week Territorial Army camp. Actually, we were seven miles or so out of Scarborough on the bleak north Yorkshire Moors. It was a blazing hot August and the resort was thronged with girls all hoping to meet good-looking lads like us. That was the theory... the practice was somewhat different!

For reasons kept as a military secret, the army refused to lay on any form of transport from the isolated training area into Scarborough in the evenings or at weekends. Perhaps it was some sort of initiative test for most of us walked or hitched; this was not so easy in those far-off days when cars were few and far between.

James Bond would have envied my sophistication, for having spent an exhilarating Saturday afternoon strolling around Scarborough, admiring the sea, the sands and the girls, I decided to get something to eat. I

Peter Flint

chose a select-looking café tucked in a corner just off the main promenade. I chose a table in the corner and, with an imperious nod of the head, summoned a fluttery waitress.

"Er... er... I'll have...er... double egg and... er... chips, beans, tomatoes, a pot of tea and bread and butter, please." What a twenty-first celebration, eh? 007 eat your heart out!

In the evening, I lost my virginity... well... nearly! The casual ease with which we had chatted with the 'bar-girls' of Hiro, Kure or Tokyo ill prepared us for the sexual mores of U.K. nineteen- fifty-four. Nowhere on Scarborough's teeming seafront were there groups of attractive young women who, for a pound, would drag you back to their rooms. True, many wore 'Kiss Me Quick!' hats but any attempt to accept this brazen offer without the preliminary ogling, whistling and backchat would have resulted, at best, in a badly bruised ego.

However, I must have learned something for the ease with which I fell into conversation with the slim, attractive girl at the fun-fair, surprised even me. We went on a few of the more hair-raising rides which gave me the excuse to put my arm around her. Then we climbed onto the Ghost Train where the mock-spooky darkness gave me enough courage to kiss her.

When we found a dark, sheltered corner near the end of the pier for some serious snogging, I was sure that this was going to celebrate my coming of age... in more ways than one! She certainly was eager and clung and strained against me in a most exciting and satisfying manner. Nowadays, the outcome would have been inevitable but in those pre-sexual revolution days one 'walked many a mile on a promise' as the saying had it!

* * *

As I have said, the government of the time cut the T.A. service to one year; then realised that this part-time military service... and a few years later, National Service itself... was too costly so it was scrapped. I did one more T.A. weekend, the details of which elude me. I can only remember a rain-soaked walk through a drab, empty, small town looking for a decent pub... a cinema... a café... a dance-hall... please god anything... it's Saturday night!

My final connections with Her Majesty's Forces were surprises and, in the circumstances, quite amusing. I received a letter telling me to hand in my army kit at the local drill-hall. I now know of many street-wise lads who only handed in useless items such as webbing, mess-tins etc, keeping greatcoats, boots and the like for their own use. I suppose I was naively honest and only too glad to rid myself of all the trappings of compulsory military service.

As requested... *ordered*... I went along to the local drill-hall to ascertain when I should report with my kit. I was greeted by the Company Sergeant Major... a being so elevated in the regular army that mere privates, such as myself, only communicated with them by shouting at the empty air. To my astonishment, he spoke to me almost as if

Peter Flint

I were a human being... not, perhaps, a good specimen but nevertheless a human being.

"Your kit, son? Yes, that's right... you do hand it in here. Have you got your A.F.1157?"

"Yes, sir," I replied.

"Good... tell you what; I'll save you the trouble of lugging it up Bath Street. I'll pop round to your house tomorrow in the car and collect your stuff."

Seems fair enough to you doesn't it? He had a car... it was only five minutes drive whereas I had to hump a great, heavy kitbag well over a mile on foot or by bus. However, I was flattered and amazed... C.S.M.s and their ilk had until recently had me racing around like a madman; polishing the studs on my boots; crawling on my belly through mud and nettles. They didn't offer to call and collect my kit... it just wasn't in their nature!

True to his word, this exception to the military rule arrived next morning and departed with the warm greatcoat I had 'dollied' so often for inspections; the B.D.s with their smooth nap and sharp creases and the 'patent-leather' boots on which I'd lavished so much care and attention over the previous twenty-four months. Now, at last, they were gone and I was blessed thought... once more a civilian!

* * *

As I have said, the glittering metropolis of Ilkeston was neither rejoicing at my departure nor my return. Anti-climax would be an exaggeration... if that is not a contradiction in terms... to describe my re-assimilation into the bosom of my family and my vast circle of adoring friends. I will refrain from including my girl friend at the time in that catalogue for obvious reasons!

I have only fairly recently realised that Der Fuhrer, Adolf Hitler... his evil philosophy and scumbag acolytes had a disastrous effect on my family life. Photos show my Mum and Dad as a good-looking, lively young married couple... they must have just moved into their brand-new, three-bedroom council house shortly after their wedding. I have very vague memories of one of them telling me that the council official handed them a bunch of keys and told them to pick which house they would like... seventy-eight years on there isn't enough 'social housing' for young families!

A few years ago on a 'down memory lane' nostalgia trip back to Ilson, as we called it, I realised that the brick, stone-capped pillars at the entrance to our small council estate upon which we lads used to climb and sit, had been built with civic pride as the sandstone carving on each one read 'Built 1933'... I was born in 1934!

My brother joined the Flint clan in 1939 just before W.W.2 broke out... my brother and my wife were both born in 1939 and I have often teased them both by suggesting that they were the cause of W.W.2... it's not really true! Dad was in a 'reserved occupation' as the textile mill where he worked was making artificial silk for parachutes. He 'did his bit' as a volunteer air-raid warden until something must have changed with his job as he was called up into the army. He eventually took part in the D-Day landings.

Suffice it to say that such a traumatic experience - a more terrifying but, in some ways similar experience to the one I have described in this book - led to the destruction, though not the break-up, of that previously new, hopeful marriage. He must have seen terrible things but he had also been shown a glimpse of the world outside our small town environment.

Mum too had her problems, brought on no doubt by worrying about my Dad; bringing up two young kids and doing a fulltime job in a large munitions factory making artillery shells. She was alone for four years until Dad was given his demob suit, a trilby hat and, I think, a small suitcase and came back to try to pick up the threads... literally and metaphorically of his/their life.

This obviously had an effect on me but much more so on my younger brother. I started work at sixteen; left to do National Service... as you have probably worked out by now, at eighteen. Like my Dad, I too saw 'the world' and, probably like Dad, felt trapped and restless when I came out of the forces. This malaise plus my left lung collapsing five times made me decide to give up the first steps on that golden ladder to mediocrity (but stability) promised by a career in the Civil Service. I sat day in day out at a desk filling in forms... five copies... each in a different colour and envisaged myself lined, grey-haired, dull (much as I am today I suppose) still filling in forms... five copies... each in a different colour until the men in white (or black!) coats came to take me away!

Adolf and Monty's mates had a definite effect on my experience, my life and thinking as I have said. Japan was a long way from 'Ilson' and mind-boggling hols in Blackpool. I have, of course, since done other things...

Apart from relatively minor tasks like helping to raise a family... now two daughters and five grand-children aged between five and twenty-two... paying off a mortgage; setting hundreds of children and young people on the educational equivalent of the yellow brick road to wealth and stardom, I have occasionally had a few spare moments to do other things...

I always say that, despite the scientific advances in medicine, agriculture and technology etc. people basically stay the same. Though life, certainly in developed countries, has become more secure, varied and interesting, offering opportunities for travelling to see our wonderful world, sadly we keep making the same mistakes.

Enough philosophising... get back to the task in hand! Where were we? Yes, I did again break out of my tiny town cocoon to...

Peter Flint

Visit my brother and his family in Up-Side-Down Land (New Zealand) for Christmas! I was fascinated by the artificial snow in shop window displays... the decorated Christmas trees and our traditional dinner - turkey, stuffing, potatoes, Christmas pudding, crackers etc, when outside the temperature must have been in the higher 20 degrees... we had a 'Barbie' (No, not an over-endowed doll! 'Barbie' is Kiwi for our more refined 'barbecue') and cracked a few tubes at a neighbours' house in the evening! On Boxing Day we had a picnic on the beach!

We hired a car and drove all round both the North and South Islands... while we were near Mount Cook on South Island, seven feet fell off the top of the mountain... it's still the highest mountain in N.Z. By the way, its collapse was entirely coincidental... it weren't me Sir... honest!

We stayed three and a half weeks then continued our round the world tour which took three and a half months and included, Beijing... Tiananmen Square... Xian... the Terra Cotta Army... snorkelling off the Great Barrier Reef... we were there at the only time of year when this two thousand mile long living organism has an orgasm! That's enough sub-aquatic porn... look it up online if you are interested.

While we were in Oz we ate a crocodile! O.K. it was only a few slices of a crocodile but it's all in the way you tell 'em! We visited Thailand, Fiji, Vancouver, Canada then flew over an incredible view of the Rockies and later floating icebergs in the Atlantic. Finally we were HOME! The airport toilets were broken and disgusting... the young woman at the information desk had obviously recently had a *charismectomy* and, when we arrived at Flint Manor the drains were blocked!

We have also visited Niagara Falls where we were not able to take the famous boat trip on 'The Maid of the Mist' as winter had lasted even longer than usual and there were blocks of ice floating below the falls. We walked over the Rainbow Bridge between Canada and America and we were refused entry to the Good Ol' U.S. of A. If you're thinking of me as a Mafia boss importing horses' heads, leading a drug smuggling ring or for that matter a gun-smuggling ring (Oh, I forgot, that would be totally surplus to requirements in America wouldn't it?)... forget it. My crime which excluded me from The Land of the Free and the Home of the Brave? We didn't have twenty dollars American in cash! We had Pounds, Canadian Dollars, Travellers' Cheques but not the equivalent of about nine quid in American currency. We were given a certificate documenting our crime and when we walked back through Canadian Customs, I asked the bored border official what I should do with it.

"Chuck it in that tray buddy!" he sighed. I wished I had kept and framed it! The certificate didn't really work or perhaps it had expired, as we later drove an R.V. from Las Vegas to the Grand Canyon along the road where one reputedly gets one's kicks... Route Sixty -Six! I had fond memories of John Wayne et al driving cattle along thet

Peter Flint

ol' Chisholm Trail towards the railhead, the saloon, the gunfight and the beautiful singer...

Actually, Thomas Chisholm... the first cowboy, was an Indian... sorry, *Native American!* Sorry to destroy your (and my) illusions... much of the landscape was very dull... I think we did glimpse ONE cow! The only iconic towering cactuses (cacti?) we might have seen were at the entrance to a little tourist town on Lake Havasu and they had been imported from Mexico... however, one of them had been stolen... cactus rustlers?

I realised we were really in America when Mike was reversing the R.V. and a guy said, in that Western drawl;

"Y'all movin'out?"

You may possibly be wondering what on earth my verbal 'holiday postcards' have to do with my experiences in the Army, well. I'll explain...

Having never travelled much more than ten miles from Ilkeston... on my first bus ride to Nottingham (eight miles) I excitedly pointed to a bulky rectangular building and asked, "Mam...Mam...is that Nottingham Castle?"...it was, in fact, John Players Cigarette Factory!... you can imagine the wonder of a five week voyage to an exotic land on the other side of the world.

When my Grandson was about six, we took him to Bristol Zoo. I said, "Look! Look at those lions!" He said, "They're not as good as those I saw in South Africa!" I think I have made my point so I will rest my case and finish... do I hear a sigh of relief?

You have all seen those horror films where the slimy bugaboo has been smashed to bits and the hero and heroine are getting down to some serious snogging. Suddenly, a disembodied head or arm of the ex-pants-filler springs up with snapping teeth or razor claws... The army's last twitch was nothing like that at all!

About six or eight months after the kindly warrant officer (I'm sure that is a contradiction in terms) had puttered off into the sunset in his mud-coloured Austin, I received an ominous, buff-coloured envelope marked... 'War Office'.

My first reaction was that the past two years had merely been a horrible dream and that these were my 'real-life' call-up papers. Thus it was that, with trembling fingers, I opened the letter to read...

"To Private P.W. Flint 22730618,

As you recently left Her Majesty's Armed Forces, will you please confirm in writing that the above is indeed your correct address. Without this information, the National Defence Plan is incomplete."

Peter Flint

I am sure that throughout this narrative you thought that I had been a less than successful, humble member of the P.B.I. (Poor Bloody Infantry) when, in actual fact, I was as vital an element in the nation's war-machine as the Fyling-Dales Early-Warning System or the Trident Nuclear Deterrent.

SLEEP SOUNDLY ENGLAND... THEY KNOW WHERE I AM!

TWO MINUTES

I wonder what thoughts
Pass through those heads
Carefully coiffured and cut
Bowed in silent churches
Cathedrals and market-squares...
'Has the dog been sick again?'
'Wish I hadn't worn these shoes'
'Is my lipstick too bright?'
'What did she mean when...?'
Some will remember...
Warm, laughing babies
Flesh ripped by flying metal
Bones and skulls smashed
With explosive hammers
A grinning, cheeky schoolboy
Screaming in his agony
Boisterous young men
Eyes now dull and staring...
Banners droop...bugles wail
Arthritic arms creak to salute
Priests, politicians spew platitudes
In reverential tones...
'Lest we forget!'
The last grain drops
Breaking the stillness
Once more......
    They are forgotten!

Peter Flint
November 11th 2009